THE PLATONIC DOCTRINES OF ALBINUS

THE PLATONIC DOCTRINES OF ALBINUS

Translated from the Greek by
Jeremiah Reedy

With an Introduction by
Jackson P. Hershbell

Phanes Press
1991

B
535
.A43
D5313
1991

DEDICATION

For Linda M.
Memor Amicitiae

98 97 96 95 94 93 92 91   5 4 3 2 1

Published by Phanes Press, PO Box 6114, Grand Rapids, MI 49516, USA.

Library of Congress Cataloging-in-Publication Data

Albinus.
    [Didaskalikos. English]
    The Platonic doctrines of Albinus / translated from the Greek by Jeremiah Reedy ; with an introduction by Jackson P. Hershbell.
       p.   cm.
    Translation of: Didaskalikos.
    Includes bibliographical references.
    ISBN 0-933999-14-3 (alk. paper) — ISBN 0-933999-15-1 (pbk. : alk. paper)
    1. Plato. 2. Neoplatonism. I. Reedy, Jeremiah. II. Title.
B535.A43D5313   1991
184—dc20   91–25598
                                                  CIP

This book is printed on alkaline paper which conforms to the permanent paper standard developed by the National Information Standards Organization.

Printed and bound in the United States

Contents

PREFACE

I am indebted to Michael Slusser of Duquesne University for calling my attention to the need for a translation of this work. It was our intention initially to work together on it, but his busy schedule and subsequent move to Pittsburgh conspired to make collaboration impossible. I am, nonetheless, very grateful to him for providing the impetus for this whole effort.

I wish to thank Mrs. M. E. Witt, widow of R. E. Witt, and Dr. Richard Witt, their son, for granting me permission to obtain from Cambridge University Library a photocopy of an unpublished translation of the *Didaskalikos* submitted by R. E. Witt along with his doctoral dissertation in 1934. G. Waller and A. E. B. Owen of the Library's staff assisted me by locating and having the copy made. It is a pleasure to express my gratitude to them. Witt's version proved to be invaluable, and readers will see from my notes the extent to which I am indebted to it.

Finally I wish to thank Barbara Molstad for typing and patiently retyping the text and helping in many other ways. Without her assistance the whole project would have been much more difficult and time-consuming. It goes without saying, however, that I alone am responsible for any errors that may have slipped through.

—JEREMIAH REEDY
ST. PAUL, MINNESOTA

INTRODUCTION

The Life and Works of Albinus

Among the many Platonists of the second century, Albinus is one of the most important. That he was highly regarded in antiquity as a philosopher is clear from several references to him. For example, he is mentioned in the *Canones* together with Gaius (his teacher), Taurus, Priscian, Proclus, Damascius, and Johannes Philoponus as one of the more useful (*chrêsimôteroi*) of Plato's commentators.[1] Proclus lists the 'superstars' (*koryphaioi*) among the Platonists who commented on Book X of the *Republic*, and Albinus' name is second after that of Numenius, and is followed by Gaius, Maximus of Nicea, Harpocration, and Porphyry.[2] Aside from two meager facts, however, nothing is known about the life of Albinus. First, the famous medical writer Galen (c. 129–199 C.E.) who had been studying in Pergamum, reports in his *De libris propiis* that around 151 C.E. he decided to continue his studies in Smyrna "because of Pelops the physician and Albinus the Platonist."[3] Second, according to the index to *Codex Parisinus graecus* 1962, Albinus published the lectures of his teacher Gaius in nine (or ten) books.[4] But exactly when or where Gaius himself taught is not known, and so the report does not help in determining Albinus' dates. From the fact, however, that he was famous enough to attract students such as Galen from afar, G. Invernizzi has plausibly concluded that he was born around the year 100 C.E.[5]

Two works of Albinus have survived intact, and these have been described by J. Dillon as "basic school handbooks," though the *Eisagôgê* is perhaps a transcript of a student's notes.[6] It consists of six short chapters, and is only four and one-half pages long in C. F. Hermann's edition. As its title suggests, the *Eisagôgê* is an introduction to Plato's dialogues (it is also called *Prologue* in some later manuscripts), and discusses their form and content.[7] There is also what is called the *Didaskalikos* by most scholars although P. Louis, following three of the earliest manuscripts, prefers the title *Epitome*.[8] This work is a systematic introduction to the philosophy of Plato in thirty-six chapters of varying length, and will be examined at greater length presently. In addition to these works, Albinus may have written commentaries on several of Plato's dialogues. Proclus, for example, refers to Albinus in his own commentaries on the *Republic* and *Timaeus*, but his remarks are not conclusive evidence that Albinus himself wrote extensively on these works.[9] There is also mention in *Codex Parisinus graecus* 1962 of a treatise *On the Doctrines of Plato* by Albinus, and the *Didaskalikos* may be a short version of this no longer extant work. Lastly, Dillon has pointed out similarities between the doctrines and terminology of Albinus and those of the author of the *Anonymous Theaetetus Commentary*, but these are not enough to prove that Albinus was the commentator.[10]

The Form and Content of the *Didaskalikos*

For centuries the *Didaskalikos* was transmitted under the false name of "Alkinoos" until it was observed by J. Freudenthal, a nineteenth-century German scholar, that this was a corruption in a minuscule manuscript for "Albinos."[11] The work was clearly intended to be an introduction to Plato's teachings, and to assist anyone interested in becoming a student of Plato and capable of discovering the meaning of his philosophy (chapter 36). Despite Albinus' own doubts about the orderliness of his work, the *Didaskalikos* is carefully organized into four parts followed by a conclusion consisting of two chapters. There is an introduction (chapters 1–3), a section on dialectic (4–6), a long section on 'theoretic philosophy' (freely translated by Louis as "The Contemplation of Being"), and nine chapters on ethics (27–34). The section on theoretic philosophy includes mathematics (7), theology (8–11) and physics (12–26) which deals with such diverse subjects as creation, the elements, the world soul, planets, stars, created gods, the human body, the senses, causes of diseases, parts of the soul, its immortality and its freedom. Under the heading of ethics, Albinus treats of the highest Good, the virtues, pleasure and pain, friendship, and finally political virtue and the various kinds of civil constitutions.

From the *Didaskalikos* emerges what H. Dörrie has called "a self-contained form of Platonism,"[12] and probably like many of his fellow Platonists, Albinus did not feel the necessity of producing original work. He had tremendous respect for Plato's wisdom, and thus perceived his task to be that of transmitting what he believed was the essence of Plato's thought in a reliable manner. Indeed, the fact that chapter 12 of the *Didaskalikos*, which concerns the Forms, seems to be a close paraphrase of remarks by Arius Didymus on the same subject (preserved in Eusebius, *Praeparatio Evangelica* XI 23, 2, and Stobaeus, *Anthologium* I 135, 19 Wachs.), suggests not necessarily that Albinus' work was a 'new edition' of Arius' *On the Doctrines of Plato*, but that the two authors may well have been using a common source regarded as providing traditional Platonic teaching.[13] In any case, it is necessary to have some understanding of Albinus' *Didaskalikos* in the history of Platonism.

The *Didaskalikos* and Platonism

Although Plato believed that the most profound doctrines do not admit of written expression and can only be the result of lifelong study (see his *Seventh Letter*, 342A ff.), this conviction did not prevent him and his successors from producing a vast number of philosophical works. Many of these, however, are lost, and except for the dialogues of Plato himself and the writings of Plutarch of Chaironeia (c. 45–120 C.E.), the *Didaskalikos* of Albinus is the only fully-preserved work of Platonism until the time of Plotinus (c. 205–270 C.E.). It is thus an important work in understanding the history of Platonism following Plato's death in 347 B.C.E.

A history of Platonism cannot be undertaken here,[14] but it is important to keep in mind that Plato's dialogues were not his last word on any subject, and that his oral teachings as reported, for example, by Aristotle in the *Metaphysics*, exercized a great influence on his followers. On the whole, however, they were not content simply to formalize or reproduce Plato's philosophy, written and unwritten, and some of them show originality in their teachings. Speusippus, for example, substituted numbers for the Forms or Ideas, and believed in a One beyond Being, and the source from which Being springs. He thus anticipated the later teachings of Plotinus. Xenocrates, another member of the Old Academy, seems to have been less original and tended to formalize Plato's thought. Yet he reduced the soul itself to number, and defined it as "self-moving number." He also defined an Idea as "the paradigmatic cause of regular natural phenomena," and so tried to rule out Ideas of artificial objects such as beds and lyres, and things contrary to nature (*physis*) such as ugliness and sickness. This became the standard definition among Platonists of the early Roman empire (Middle Platonism), and appears in Albinus' *Didaskalikos* (chapter 9).

For a time the Academy was to abandon its positive metaphysical teaching, especially when attacking the Stoics, and under Arcesilaus (c. 316–241 B.C.E.) and Carneades (c. 214–129 B.C.E.), there was a denial of the possibility of knowledge, and the New or Sceptical Academy tended to base itself on Socrates' famous affirmation of ignorance: "I know that I do not know." But with Antiochus of Ascalon (c. 130–68 B.C.E.) there was a clear break with the scepticism of Carneades and his own teacher, Philo of Larissa, and a return to the more positive teaching of the Old Academy. Antiochus, however, went considerably beyond his predecessors in maintaining that Aristotle was a Platonist, at least in one phase of his thinking, and that the Peripatos was essentially identical with the Academy despite its modification of Plato's ethical theory. He was also convinced that Stoic philosophy was derived from the Old Academy, and accepted, for example, the Stoic doctrine of certainty, 'the cognitive presentation' or 'impression' (*phantasia katalêptikê*).

Given, then, Antiochus' attempts to reconcile or even to identify Platonic doctrine with Peripatetic and Stoic, it is not surprising that similar tendencies appear in Albinus a little more than a century later. Thus, for example, at the end of chapter four of the *Didaskalikos* he makes a distinction between *theoria* and *praxis* which is Aristotelian, and also uses the Stoic term *physike ennoia*, 'natural' or 'innate concept.' He also adapts the Aristotelian categories as Platonic (chapter 6), and his early definition of wisdom (*sophia*) as "knowledge of things divine and human" (chapter 1) is essentially Stoic in formulation.

Clearly between Plato's death and Albinus' *Didaskalikos* a number of changes had taken place both within and without the Academy, and yet Platonism remained strongly tied to a tradition based on respect for the wisdom of Plato. Plato's teachings on various subjects sometimes seem ambiguous, for example, on whether the cosmos had a beginning in time, and he often does not appear to have reached any final conclusions, but left it to his followers to think out matters for themselves. And yet Plato formulated the major problems with which his followers were concerned, for example, the nature of the Ideas and their relationship to one another and to the perceptible world, the purpose of life and the achievement of 'well-being' (*eudaimonia*), and provided guideposts, as it were, for thinking about these problems. Some later Platonists such as Albinus would have even regarded Plato as anticipating, or at least alluding to everything which Aristotelian logic, for example, and Stoic ethics later unfolded. For Albinus, philosophizing was only an explication of Plato's thought,[15] and he was not especially aware of any breaks in the tradition between Plato and himself, a tradition which was based not only on Plato's written and oral teachings, but also on the interpretations of followers such as Speusippus, Xenocrates, or Antiochus.

In composing the *Didaskalikos* Albinus was not striving for originality, for he regarded the work simply as an "introduction to the teachings of Plato," and as making it "possible for anyone to become a student of Plato and consequently be capable of discovering the meaning of the rest of his teachings" (chapter 36). The *Didaskalikos* was thus propaedeutic and not meant to be a complete or definitive exposition of Plato's philosophy. Given Albinus' intent, then, it is not likely that much in the work is original. But Albinus' apparent lack of originality should not detract from the fact that his work is extremely valuable as a sketch of Platonism in the second century C.E.

The *Didaskalikos* Today

For a scholar or interested reader of today, the *Didaskalikos* provides good insights into the thinking of the period between Antiochus of Ascalon and Plotinus, a period commonly known as Middle Platonism. It shows that there was a strong tendency to incorporate teachings of the Old Academy, for example, Xenocrates' definition of an Idea, and those of Aristotle and his school. Chapters five and six, for example, are an exposition of later Peripatetic logic presented so as to make it seem Platonic. Similarly in his discussion of matter in chapter eight, Albinus uses the Aristotelian term *hyle*, and describes matter as "body in potency." Even in chapter ten, perhaps the best-known section of the *Didaskalikos*, which deals with the nature of God, Albinus' notion of a primal God who is motionless, but acting on the cosmos as "the object of desire arouses desire while remaining motionless itself," is very reminiscent of Aristotle's prime mover in *Metaphysics* XII. Yet in his discussion of God, he uses three terms, "without need" (*autoteles*), "eternally perfect" (*aeiteles*), and "all perfect" (*panteles*), which are not found together in any surviving text, and of which one, *aeiteles*, is found nowhere else.[16]

It is also in chapter ten that Albinus shows a knowledge of mystical theology, and anticipates Plotinus.[17] The epithets of God mentioned previously do not define, but simply name God. Albinus then discussed three ways of describing God, and one of these involves removing attributes of God, a procedure later known as

the *via negativa*. Two other ways of thinking about God are by
Analogy for which he uses as an example the simile of the sun
(*Republic* VI), and by Anagôgê (leading upwards) for which he
adduces Diotima's famous speech in the *Symposium*. Indeed,
throughout the *Didaskalikos*, Albinus not only shows familiarity
with Plato's written works, but draws heavily from them. Mathematics, for example, is discussed in chapter seven in terms taken
from *Republic* VII (525B ff.), and the *Timaeus* dominates chapters
twelve to twenty-two with their account of the physical world,
daimones, and the human soul. Many other examples of Albinus'
reliance on Plato could be cited, for example, in chapter twenty-
eight where the goal of becoming like God is essentially a formulation
found in *Theaetetus* 176B and is one of the dominant themes of
Middle Platonism.[18]

In conclusion, Albinus' *Didaskalikos* is an extremely valuable
document for understanding the history of Platonism and anticipates some of the mystical theology of later centuries. It shows an
individual who is very devoted to what he believes were the
fundamental teachings of the divine Plato, and who is eager to win
disciples. In some ways, Albinus' mentality is not so different from
that of any well-educated early Christian attempting to transmit
the teachings of a Saviour already interpreted and selected by Jesus'
followers. Both were, after all, living in what E. R. Dodds called "an
age of anxiety."[19]

—JACKSON P. HERSHBELL

NOTES

1. The *Canones* was edited by W. Cronert (Königsberg, 1911). See H. Dörrie, "Albinos," in *Paulys Realencyclopädie der Classischen Altertumswissenschaft, Supplementband* XII (Stuttgart: A. Druckenmüller, 1970), col. 15. Dörrie's article is an excellent introduction to Albinus.

2. In Plato, *Republic* II 96, 11 cited by Dörrie, "Albinos," col. 15.

3. Cited in Dörrie, "Albinos," col. 14.

4. "Albinos," col. 14.

5. Giuseppe Invernizzi, *Il Didaskalikos di Albino e il Mediplatonismo* (Rome: Abete, 1976), II, 3.

6. See John Dillon, *The Middle Platonists* (London: Duckworth, 1977), 268 and 304. Dillon notes that for Albinus, "the study of the dialogues of Plato is virtually coextensive with higher education in general."

7. In the *Eisagôgê* the dialogues are distinguished according to type or kind: a) dialogues of instruction (*hypohêgêtikos*) and b) dialogues of inquiry (*zêtêtikos*), and a course of reading is prescribed which starts with *Alcibiades I* (on knowledge of the self) and ends with the *Timaeus* (on the cosmos and divinity).

8. P. Louis, *Épitomé* (Paris: Budé, 1945), xii.

9. Dillon, *Middle Platonists*, 269–270.

10. *Middle Platonists*, 270–271.

11. See Dörrie, "Albinos," col. 14.

12. "Albinos," col. 21: "ein in sich geschlossener Platonismus."

13. See Dillon's discussion, *The Middle Platonists*, 269 and 286. The similarities between the beginning of chapter twelve and Arius Didymus's *On the Doctrines of Plato* are not enough to prove that Arius' work was the basis for Albinus' entire *Didaskalikos*.

14. Besides Dillon's *The Middle Platonists*, the relevant chapters in *The Cambridge History of Later Greek and Early Medieval Thought*, ed. A. H. Armstrong (Cambridge, England: Cambridge University Press, repr.

1980) are well worth reading also.

15. Dörrie, "Albinos," col. 21, considers Albinus' work an *explicatio Platonis*. I am indebted to Dörrie's remarks here and elsewhere in assessing Albinus' "originality."

16. See Dillon, *Middle Platonists*, 283.

17. E. R. Dodds, in a brief discussion of Plotinus' mysticism, remarks, that "he relies on the three traditional approaches to the knowledge of God which were already listed by Albinus a century earlier." See his *Pagan and Christian in an Age of Anxiety* (Cambridge, England: Cambridge University Press, 1965), 87.

18. See Dillon, *The Middle Platonists*, esp. 43–45.

19. See note 17 above.

DIDASKALIKOS OF ALBINUS

1

May the following serve as a summary of Plato's principal teachings. Philosophy is a striving after wisdom or a release and a redirecting of the soul from the body that occurs when we turn ourselves to the intelligible world and the things which truly are.[1] Wisdom is knowledge of things divine and human. The word 'philosopher' is derived from 'philosophy' as 'musician' is from 'music.' The philosopher must in the first place have a natural penchant for doctrines which can prepare him and lead him to knowledge of Being which is intelligible and does not change and is not in a state of flux. Next the philosopher must have clung to the truth with desire, and he must in no way entertain falsehood.[2] In addition he must be temperate by nature, as it were, and naturally restrained with respect to the passionate part of the soul. For the one who aims at learning to relate to the things which are and directs his striving towards them would not be an admirer of pleasures.[3] The person who is going to be a philosopher must also have an open mind, for there is no greater obstacle than pettiness of mind for a soul that is destined to contemplate things divine and human. He must also have a natural penchant for justice and, for that matter, for truth, freedom and temperance. He should also have an aptitude for learning and a good memory,[4] for these are also characteristic of the philosopher. When these noble qualities coincide with the right kind of education and a proper upbringing,

---

1. Cf. *Phaedo* 67d, 80e; *Republic* 521c.
2. *Republic* 485c.
3. *Republic* 485d.
4. *Republic* 535a-536a and 486c.

they render a person perfect as regards virtue; if, on the other hand, they are neglected, they become the source of great evils. Plato was thus accustomed to designate these talents with the same names as the virtues temperance, courage and justice.[5]

2

There are two ways of life, the contemplative and the active. The chief object of the contemplative life is knowledge of the truth, while that of the active life consists in doing those things indicated by reason. The contemplative life holds the place of honor; the active life is a consequence of it and is an absolute necessity. That this is so should become clear from what follows. Contemplation is an activity of the mind contemplating the intelligibles. Action is the activity of the rational soul operating through the body. The soul, when it contemplates the divine and the thoughts of the divine, is said to experience bliss, and this experience is called 'wisdom,'[6] which one could say is nothing else but assimilation to the divine.[7] Hence such an activity would be worthy of choice, honorable, most to be aspired to and most appropriate for us; it lies freely in our power to possess, and it forms the end which is set before us.[8] Action, however, and the active life, being accomplished by means of the body, can be interfered with. Their performance is demanded by what we see in the contemplative life, calling for application to human conduct.[9] The serious man[10] will turn to public affairs whenever he sees that they are being poorly managed by others. Thus he will consider serving in the military, serving on a jury, or going on an embassy if circumstances require it. But he

---

5. *Republic* 536a, *Meno* 88a, b.
6. φρόνησις. See *Phaedrus* 247d and *Phaedo* 79b.
7. *Theaetetus* 176b.
8. "freely...before us." Witt.
9. "Their...conduct," Witt.
10. ὁ σπουδαῖος, "The sage" Witt.

considers what concerns the establishment of laws and the constitution of civil life and education of the young as the best activities
in the practical life and to be preferred in this area. From what has
been said we see that it is fitting for the philosopher never to desist
from contemplation but always to foster and increase it and to
approach the practical life as something secondary.

3

According to Plato, the philosopher's pursuit rests on three
things: on the contemplation and understanding of things that
are,[11] on doing what is right, and on reflecting on reason. The
knowledge of 'what is' is called Theoretic philosophy; that which
concerns what is to be done is called Ethics;[12] and that concerned
with reasoning Dialectic.[13] The last is subdivided into Division,
Definition, Induction and Syllogistics. Syllogistics, in turn, is
subdivided into the Demonstrative, which deals with the necessary
syllogism; the Tentative, which is seen in the case of the probable
syllogism; and thirdly the Rhetorical, which deals with the
enthymeme, the so-called imperfect syllogism, and also with soph-
ism. Rhetoric is not the philosopher's chief concern but it is
necessary. One branch of Ethics can be viewed as dealing with
morals, the second part with the management of the household and
the third with the city and its survival. Of these the first is called
Morals, the second Economics and the last Politics. That part of
Theoretic philosophy that treats of what is unmoved, of first causes
and of such things as are divine, is called Theology. The part dealing
with the motion of stars, their courses and periodic returns and the
structure of the cosmos, is called Physics. That which employs
geometry and other branches of mathematics is Mathematics. Such

11. *Republic* 582c.
12. *Politicus* 259c, d.
13. *Sophistes* 253d.

then is the division and the classification of the branches of philosophy. We must speak first about dialectical theory as it appealed to Plato and first of all about the criterion.

4

Since there is something that judges and something that is judged, there would also be that which results from them which one might call judgment. One might properly call judgment the criterion, but more commonly this term is applied to that which makes the judgment. This is twofold: that by which what is judged is judged, i.e. the agent, and that through which it is judged, i.e. the instrument. The former would be our mind, the latter, through which, would be the natural instrument that judges principally truths but also secondarily falsehood. This is nothing else but natural reason.[14] Obviously the philosopher by whom affairs are judged could be called the judge, but reason through which truth is judged (which we have called an instrument) is also a judge. Now reason is twofold. One type is certain and precise but is completely incomprehensible to us; the other is infallible regarding the knowledge of things. Of these two the former is within the power of a god but impossible for a human being. The latter is possible even for a human.[15] Human reason in turn is twofold: one part deals with intelligibles, the other sensibles. The first, dealing with intelligibles, is understanding and scientific reason;[16] the other, which deals with sensibles, is doxastic reason and opinion.[17] Because of this, scientific reason has certainty and stability in as much as it relates to what is certain and stable. Persuasive[18] and doxastic reason is characterized

14. λόγος φυσικός, "natural discursive reason" Witt.
15. *Timaeus* 51e.
16. ἐπιστήμη καὶ ἐπιστημονικός.
17. δοξαστκός τε καὶ δόξα, "reason operating as opinion" Witt. See *Republic* 476c and ff. 'Doxastic reason' is reason based on sensible appearances rather than scientific principles.
18. πιθανός.

rather by probability because it deals with what is unstable. The starting points of understanding which is concerned with intelligibles, and opinion which deals with sensibles, are intellection and sense perception respectively. Sense perception is an effect on the soul mediated through the body which presents the report primarily of the faculty affected.[19] Whenever an impression corresponding to a sensation arises in the soul through the senses (which is what perception is) and does not fade away over time but persists and is preserved, its preservation is called memory.[20] Opinion is a combination of memory and perception.[21] For whenever we encounter some perceptible object for the first time and perception of it takes place in us and from this comes memory, and then we encounter the same object of perception again, we compare the preexisting memory with the perception arising from the second encounter, and we say to ourselves, 'This is Socrates' or 'a horse' or 'fire' or something similar. This is what is called opinion, as we combine the preexisting memory with the fresh perception. When these two, after being compared to one another, agree, we have a true opinion; when they disagree, we have a false opinion. If someone with an image of Socrates in mind meets Plato and thinks because of some resemblance he is meeting Socrates again, then taking the perception of Plato to be that of Socrates he combines it with the memory he has of Socrates, a false opinion results. That [medium] in which memory and perception take place Plato likens to a lump of wax.[22] When the soul remodels in thought those things which were received from perception and memory and looks at them just as it looked at the originals from which they were produced, Plato calls this 'representation,' and sometimes 'imagination.'[23] Plato defines thought as the dialogue of the soul

19. *Timaeus* 43c, 45d.
20. *Theaetetus* 192a.
21. *Philebus* 38b.
22. *Theaetetus* 191c.
23. ἀναζωγράφησιν...καὶ φαντασίαν. On the first see *Philebus* 39b; on *phantasia* see *Theaetetus* 161e and *Sophist* 263e.

with itself, and speech is the stream from the soul flowing through
the mouth with sound.[24] Intellection is the activity of the mind as
it contemplates the primary intelligibles. It appears to be twofold:
one kind took place before the soul entered the body as it contemplated the intelligibles; the other after its entry into the body. The
first of these which took place prior to the soul's incarnation is
intellection, strictly speaking. Once the soul is in the body, what
was formerly called intellection is now called natural or innate
conception,[25] in as much as it is intellection of a sort stored up in the
soul. Thus when we say that intellection is the starting point of
scientific reason, we do not mean what was just mentioned but that
which occurred when the soul existed apart from the body which,
as we said, was called intellection but now "natural conception."
Plato also calls natural conception both 'knowledge pure and
simple'[26] and the 'soul's plumage,'[27] and sometimes 'remembrance.'
Natural and scientific reason which exist in us naturally are con-
stituted of these pure and simple ideas. Thus since there is both
scientific and doxastic reason and since there is both intellection
and perception, there exist also those things which give rise to
them, namely the intelligibles and perceptibles. And since some
intelligibles are primary, namely the Ideas, and some are secondary, namely the forms which inhere in matter and are inseparable
from it, intellection will also be of two kinds, the one of primary
intelligibles, the other of secondary ones. Again, among perceptibles
some are primary, for example qualities such as whiteness, and
others are accidents of bodies,[28] such as the whitish hue in the
colored object.[29] In addition to these there are composite bodies[30]

24. *Sophist* 263e.
25. φυσικὴ ἔννοια.
26. ἐπιστήμη ἁπλῆ.
27. *Phaedrus* 246e.
28. τὰ δὲ κατὰ συμβεβηκός, "accidents of bodies" Dillon; "others exist per accidens" Witt.
29. "whitish...object" Witt.
30. ἄθροισμα, l'agregat concret, Louis; congeries, Witt.

such as fire and honey. Thus perception of primary perceptibles will be called primary, and perception of secondary perceptibles secondary. Intellection judges the primary intelligibles not without scientific reason[31] intuitively and not discursively, and scientific reason judges the secondary intelligibles not without intellection. Sense perception judges the primary and secondary perceptibles not without doxastic reason. Doxastic reason judges the composite body not without perception. Since the intelligible world is the first intelligible, and the perceptible world is a congeries, intellection judges the intelligible world with reason (that is, not without reason); doxastic reason judges the perceptible world not without perception. We have seen that there is contemplation and action; right reason does not judge in the same way those matters that fall within the sphere of contemplation and those that require action, but in the area of contemplation it considers what is true and what is not while in the sphere of action it looks to what would be appropriate, what would be out of place and what should be done. For, thanks to the innate conception we have of what is beautiful and good, we judge whether such and such is so or not, using reason and referring to our innate concepts as established criteria.

5

Plato believes the most basic task of Dialectic to be, first, to consider the essence of everything and then the accidents. Dialectic investigates everything that is either from above (i.e. *a priori*), by means of division and definition, or from below (*a posteriori*), through analysis. It investigates accidents that belong to essences either through induction, which proceeds from what they entail, or by syllogism, which proceeds from what entails them.[32] Thus according to this account the parts of Dialectic are Division, Definition,

---

31. "not without scientific reason." See Dillon p. 274.
32. "which...entails them." Witt.

Analysis, Induction and Syllogistic. Now then, Division is, on the one hand, of genus into species and on the other of the whole into parts, as for example when we separate the soul into the rational and passionate elements, and again the passionate part into the spirited and appetitive parts.[33] Another example is the division of a word into its meanings as when one and the same noun is applied to many things. There is also the division of accidents according to their subjects as when we speak of goods of the soul, of the body and of external goods, and there is the division of subjects according to their accidents as when we speak of people as good or bad or in between. Now we must first divide the genus into its species in order to discern what each thing is *per se* in its essence. This would be impossible without a definition, which is produced from division in the following way. When a thing is to be given a definition, one must first discover the genus, for example 'animal' for the human being, then divide it according to its appropriate differentiae[34] going down to the species; for example, animal is divided into rational and irrational, and rational into mortal and immortal. Adding then the appropriate differentiae to the genus, the definition of man results. There are three forms of analysis. The first is an ascent from the sensible things to the first intelligibles. The second is an ascent by means of proofs and demonstration to the premises that are indemonstrable and without a middle term. The third type rises *ex hypothesi* to non-hypothetical principles.[35] The first type of analysis goes something like this: From the beautiful in bodies we pass to the beautiful in souls, and from there to the beautiful in customs, hence to the beautiful in laws, then to the vast sea of beauty. Proceeding in this manner, we discover finally Beauty

---

33. *Republic* 436a, b and *Phaedrus* passim. I translate τὸ παθητικόν "passionate part," τὸ θυμικόν "spirited" and τὸ ἐπιθυμητικόν "appetitive." Another possibility instead of "spirited" would be "irascible" and instead of "appetitive" "desiderative" or "concupiscible," for τὸ παθητικόν Witt prefers "affectible."

34. προσεχεῖς διαφοράς, "appropriate differentiae," Witt.

35. *Republic* 510b and 511b.

itself.[36] An example of the second type of analysis is this: One must first grant that which is to be proved and then consider what truths are prior to it; then one establishes these working backwards from the consequences to what is prior until we arrive at what is primary and agreed upon by all. Beginning with this, we move downward to what is in question using the method of synthesis. For example, suppose I ask if the soul is immortal;[37] after granting this, I ask if it is perpetually in motion. After proving this I ask if that which is perpetually moving is self-moving. Again after proving this, I consider whether that which is self-moving is a principle of movement, and then whether the principle is uncreated. This is posited as something generally agreed upon, the uncreated being also indestructible. Beginning with this as something evident, I construct the following proof: If it is a first principle, it is something uncreated and indestructible. That which is self-moving is a principle of motion; the soul is self-moving; therefore the soul is indestructible.[38] Analysis *ex hypothesi* goes as follows: A person questioning something posits that very thing, then considers what follows from this supposition; after this, if it is necessary to justify this hypothesis, one posits another hypothesis and asks if the thing previously posited is a consequence of the new hypothesis. One does this until he comes to some non-hypothetical principle. Induction is any logical process that proceeds from like to like or from particulars to universals. Induction is extremely useful for stirring up our innate concepts.

6

There are two kinds of propositions. One is affirmative, the other negative. An example of an affirmative proposition is "Socrates is

36. See *Symposium* 210 ff.
37. See *Phaedrus* 245c, d, e.
38. *Phaedrus* 245c.

walking." An example of a negative one is "Socrates is not walking." Of affirmative and negative propositions one is of the universal, the other of the particular. An example of a particular proposition is: "Such and such a pleasure is a good." "Such and such a pleasure is not a good" is an example of the negative. An example of a universal proposition would be this: "Every shameful thing is an evil." "No shameful thing is a good" would be the negative. Some propositions are categorical, some hypothetical. Simple propositions are categorical, for example "Every just thing is beautiful." Hypothetical ones are those which reveal a consequence or a contradiction. Plato also makes use of the syllogistic method when he is disproving or proving something. He disproves falsehood, on the one hand, through critical inquiry, and he proves the truth through instruction of one sort or another. The syllogism is an argument in which, certain things having been posited, something different from what was posited follows necessarily from the premises. Some syllogisms are categorical, some are hypothetical and some mixed. Categorical syllogisms are those whose premises and conclusions are simple propositions; hypothetical are those with hypothetical propositions while mixed are those that combine the two. Plato uses demonstrative syllogisms in the expository dialogues; he uses probable ones against the sophists and the young, and eristic ones against those who are particularly argumentative, such as Euthydemus and Hippias. There are three categorical figures: First, that in which the middle term is the predicate of one premise and the subject of the other; secondly, that in which the middle term is the predicate of both premises; and thirdly, that in which the middle term is the subject of both premises. (By terms I mean the parts of the propositions; for example in the proposition 'Man is an animal,' 'Man' and 'animal' are terms.) Plato uses all three figures for arguments in the form of questions and answers. Here is an example of one in the first figure from the *Alcibiades*:[39] "Just things

---

39. *Alcibiades* 115 ff.

are beautiful. Beautiful things are good. Ergo, just things are good." In the *Parmenides*[40] we find one in the second figure: "That which has no parts is neither straight nor round. That which participates in form is either straight or round. Ergo, that which has no parts does not participate in form." In the same dialogue there is one in the third figure: "That which participates in form has qualities. That which participates in form is limited. Therefore that which has qualities is limited." We find hypothetical syllogisms in an interrogative form in many dialogues, but especially in the *Parmenides*:[41] "If the one does not have parts, neither has it beginning nor middle nor end. If it has neither beginning nor middle nor end, it has no limit. If it has no limit, it does not participate in shape. If, therefore, the one has no parts, it does not participate in shape." The second hypothetical figure, which most people call the third and in which the middle term comes after the extreme terms in both premises, Plato develops interrogatively thus: "If the one does not have parts, it is neither straight nor round. If it participates in shape, it is either straight or round. If then it has no parts, it does not participate in shape."[42] In the *Phaedo* Plato gives us an example of the third figure (which some call the second). In this figure the middle term precedes both extreme terms:[43] "If having knowledge of equality, we do not forget it, we know it. But if we forget it, we recover it by recollection." Finally, he has examples of mixed syllogisms which proceed either in constructive sequence or in destructive sequence.[44] An example of the former runs thus:[45] "If the one is a whole and is determinate, having beginning, middle and end, it also participates in shape." The antecedent is true; so also the consequent.[46] From this example one can observe how mixed syllogisms which refute by way

40. *Parmenides* 145b.
41. *Parmenides* 137d.
42. *Parmenides* 145b.
43. *Phaedo* 72e and 75c, translation after Witt.
44. "Which...destructive sequence." Witt.
45. *Parmenides* 145a.
46. Witt et al. believe they have discerned a lacuna here. I follow Louis.

of the consequence differ from earlier types. If, then, a person knows precisely the faculties of the soul, the differences among the people, and the types of arguments which appeal to such and such a soul, if one grasps quickly what sort of person can be persuaded by what sorts of arguments, and if one seizes the right opportunity to practice his skill, such a person will be the perfect orator and his rhetoric will be justly called the science of speaking well. We will also find in the *Euthydemus*, if we read it carefully, Plato's outline of sophisms. There he tells us which fallacies are verbal, which are independent of language and what the solutions to them are. In the *Parmenides* and other dialogues Plato deals with the ten categories while he explores the whole subject of etymology in the *Cratylus*. Putting it quite simply, Plato is very competent in this area, and he is an admirer of definition and division which together make manifest especially well the power of dialectic. I shall try to capture the spirit of the *Cratylus* in what follows: He poses the question whether words exist by nature or by convention. His position is that the appropriateness of words is a matter of convention, not purely nor accidentally, however, but in such a way that the convention is a consequence of the nature of the thing. The appropriateness of a word is, in fact, nothing but the accord of the convention with the nature of the thing.[47] For neither haphazard convention nor nature, that is the earliest utterance, is sufficient for the correctness of a word. What is needed is a combination of the two so that the word for each thing is appropriate to its nature. For if one imposed the first word to come to mind on the first thing encountered, it would not, I assume, give the correct meaning, for example if we called a man a horse. Speaking is a unique human act;[48] hence the person who speaks haphazardly will not speak correctly. One's speech must be in accord with the nature of the references. Now since naming is a part of speaking just as a noun is a part of speech, correct

47. *Cratylus* 422d, 428e.
48. *Cratylus* 387b, c.

and incorrect naming will depend not upon some random convention but upon the natural appropriateness of the word for the thing. The best name-giver will be that person who is able to signify the nature of the thing through the name coined for it. The name is an instrument which refers to a thing chosen not arbitrarily but appropriately for its nature.[49] By means of words we instruct one another about things, and we distinguish one thing from another.[50] Thus the name is an instrument designed for teaching and distinguishing the essence of each thing as the shuttle is designed to make cloth.[51] The correct use of words pertains to Dialectic. For, as the weaver will use the shuttle correctly since he understands its function although it was made by a carpenter, so too the dialectician will use the word coined by the name-giver.[52] The construction of a rudder depends upon the carpenter; its correct use is up to the pilot. So the name-giver will make correct use of the convention if he acts in the presence of the dialectician, the person who has knowledge of the essence of objects.

7

So much for Dialectic; let us now speak about Theory.[53] We have already said that one part of it is Theology, another Physics and the third Mathematics. We have also said that the goal of Theology is knowledge of first causes which are supreme and primordial. The goal of Physics is to discover the nature of the universe, to learn what sort of animal man is and what place he occupies in the universe, and whether God exercises providence over everything, and if there are other gods subordinate to Him, and finally what the relationship is between humans and gods. The object of Mathematics is to examine

---

49. *Cratylus* 389a.
50. *Cratylus* 388b.
51. *Cratylus* 389a.
52. *Cratylus* 390b, c.
53. "contemplative knowledge," Witt.

the nature of planes and solids and how they are related to both
motion and locomotion. Let us first set forth briefly the theory[54] of
Mathematics. Mathematics was adopted by Plato because it sharpens
the intellect,[55] touches the soul and promotes accuracy in the
investigation of reality. That part of Mathematics that deals with
numbers, far from forming an accidental relation to the ascent to
being,[56] virtually frees us from the error and ignorance entailed by
sensibilia,[57] assisting us to arrive at the knowledge of what truly is.
It also has value in wartime since it teaches us the principles of
tactics.[58] Geometry is also very valuable for knowledge of the Good,
provided one does not study it for practical ends but uses it to
ascend towards what always is, not wasting time with what comes
to be and passes away.[59] Solid geometry is also very useful, for after
studying two dimensions the study of three follows naturally.[60]
Equally valuable is Astronomy,[61] the fourth branch of Mathematics; it enables us to observe the movements of the stars and of the
heavens and also to contemplate the Creator of the night and day
and of the months and years. The heavenly bodies will incline us to
seek the Creator of the universe because of a natural propensity we
have. We will use mathematics as the basis and foundation with
which to begin. We shall also cultivate Music, directing our
hearing towards these same objects.[62] For, just as the eyes were
made for astronomy, the ears were made for harmony, and just as
by applying our minds to astronomy we are led from visible things
to invisible and intelligible reality, so also by listening to harmonious music are we raised from what is audible to those things which

54. "speculative method," Witt.
55. *Republic* 525b-526c.
56. "far from...relation" Witt.
57. "error...sensibilia," Witt.
58. *Republic* 525b.
59. *Republic* 526c, d, e.
60. *Republic* 528a, b.
61. *Republic* 527d.
62. *Republic* 530d.

can be contemplated by the mind alone. Unless we pursue our mathematical studies in this way, research concerning these matters will be incomplete and devoid of benefit and value. We must pass quickly from what is visible and audible to those things which are made visible to the soul by reason alone. The study of Mathematics, in sum, constitutes a kind of prelude to the vision of ultimate reality;[63] and geometry, arithmetic and their related fields, while striving to grasp reality, only dream of it, for they are unable to have a waking view of it because they are ignorant of first principles and of the system which they constitute.[64] Nonetheless, as we have stated, they are very useful. Hence Plato refused to grant to Mathematics the name of science. It is natural, however, for the dialectical method to rise from geometrical hypotheses to first principles that are non-hypothetical. Thus Plato called Dialectic a science, but Mathematics he called neither opinion, because it is clearer than sensibilia,[65] nor science, because it is more obscure than the first intelligibles. According to him, opinion is of bodies, science of first intelligibles, and understanding[66] of mathematical objects. He also asserts the existence of belief and conjecture;[67] belief is of sensibilia and conjecture of images and copies.[68] Dialectic thus is more powerful than Mathematics since it deals with objects which are divine and immutable. It, therefore, occupies a higher place than Mathematics, being as it were a capstone or safeguard for all other studies.

8

Next in order let us speak of the first principles and precepts of

---

63. *Republic* 531d.
64. "the system...constitute," Witt; *Republic* 533b, c.
65. *Republic* 533d.
66. διάνοια.
67. *Republic* 534a.
68. *Republic* 510a.

Theology. We shall begin at the top with the most basic problems and descend from there considering the origin of the cosmos and concluding with the creation and nature of human beings. Let us speak first about matter. Plato calls matter a recipient of impressions,[69] a universal receptacle,[70] a nurse,[71] a mother,[72] space,[73] and a substrate that is tangible and "apprehensible by a kind of bastard reasoning by the aid of non-sensation."[74] Its peculiar nature is such that, having the nature of a nurse, it receives the whole of creation by bearing all forms since it is *per se* without shape,[75] without quality and without form. Being kneaded and formed like a lump of wax, it is shaped by these since it has neither shape of its own nor qualities. For it would not be well suited to receive diverse impressions and forms unless it were itself without qualities and free from those forms which it is destined to receive. We see that men who manufacture fragrant ointments from oil use oil that is as odorless as possible, and craftsmen who desire to model figures of wax or clay render the material smooth first and as shapeless as possible.[76] It is convenient, then, that matter, the all-receiver—if it is to receive all forms—be without qualities and form in order to receive the forms. As such it would be neither corporeal nor incorporeal; it would be a body in potency just as we understand bronze to be a statue in potency because after receiving the form it will be a statue.

9

Granted that matter is a first principle, Plato admits the existence

69. *Timaeus* 50c.
70. *Timaeus* 51a.
71. *Timaeus* 49a, 52d, 88d.
72. *Timaeus* 50d, 51a.
73. *Timaeus* 52a, d.
74. "apprehensible...non-sensation." *Timaeus* 52b, Bury (Loeb).
75. *Timaeus* 50d-51a.
76. *Timaeus* 50e.

of still others, for example the paradigmatic first principle, that is the Ideas. There is also God, the Father and Cause of all things. The Idea is, in relation to God, His thought;[77] in relation to us, it is the first intelligible; in relation to matter, it is measure; in relation to the sensible world, it is a model; in relation to itself it is reality. For in general everything that is done with deliberation must be done with respect to something else[78] as if each thing proceeded from something else. For example, my image comes from me; the model must have preexisted. Whether or not the model exists externally, each artist possesses within himself the model and imposes its form upon the matter. Platonists define the Idea as an eternal model of things that exist naturally. Most of them do not like the notion that there are Ideas of artifacts such as shields or lyres, nor of abnormal things such as fevers or the cholera,[79] nor of individuals such as Socrates and Plato, nor of worthless things such as dirt and straw,[80] nor of relative notions such as 'greater' and 'superior.' For Ideas are the thoughts of God which are eternal and perfect in themselves. Platonists justify their belief that Ideas exist in the following way: whether God is mind or a being endowed with mind, He will have thoughts, and they will be eternal and immutable. But if this is so, the Ideas exist. Second, if matter is unmeasured by its very nature, it must acquire measure from something else which is superior to it and immaterial. If the antecedent is admitted, the consequent follows, and in that case the Ideas exist and are immaterial sorts of measures. Again, if the cosmos is not such as it is as a result of chance, it has been generated not only out of something but also by something, and this is not yet enough—it has been generated according to a pattern of something. Could that after which it has been made be anything but the Idea? Hence the

77. "Cette conception de l'Idée n'est pas platonicienne." Louis.
78. i.e. the formal cause.
79. *Republic* 466d.
80. *Parmenides* 130c.

Ideas would exist. Moreover, if intelligence differs from true opinion,[81] then the realm of the intelligible differs from that of opinion. If this is so, there must be intelligible objects which are different from the objects of opinion. Thus there would be primary intelligibles just as there would be primary sensibles. If this is so, the Ideas exist. But, as a matter of fact, intelligence does differ from true opinion. Thus the Ideas exist.

10

We must now discuss the third principle. Plato considered it almost ineffable, but in dealing with it we may proceed in the following way: If intelligibles exist and they are neither sensible nor do they participate in the sensible world but in certain first intelligibles, then there exist first intelligibles in an absolute sense[82] just as there are also first sensibles.[83] Grant the antecedent and the consequent follows. In as much as humans are filled with impressions from sensation, they do not know the intelligibles in a pure manner. Thus, whenever they propose to contemplate the intelligible, they have the sensible imagined with it and often add, for example, size, shape and color. The gods, on the other hand, know intelligibles absolutely and in an unmixed manner apart from any sense perception. Since mind is superior to soul, and mind in act knowing all things simultaneously and eternally is superior to mind in potentiality, and since the cause of this and of whatever else might exist above these is still more noble, this would be the primal God, the cause of the everlasting activity of the mind of the whole heaven. Although without motion Himself, the primal God acts upon the cosmos as the sun does on the sight of one looking at it or

---

81. *Timaeus* 51d.
82. πρῶτα νοητὰ ἁπλᾶ, premiers intelligibiles dans un sens absolu, Louis; "intelligibles...that are primary and simple." Witt.
83. See above Chapters 4 and 9.

as the object of desire arouses desire while remaining motionless itself. Thus also will this mind set in motion the mind of the whole heaven. Since the primal intelligence is supremely beautiful, the object of its knowledge must also be supremely beautiful, but nothing is more beautiful than God. God must, therefore, contemplate eternally Himself and His own thoughts,[84] and this activity is Idea. The primal God is eternal, ineffable, self-sufficient, that is without need, eternally perfect, that is perfect for all times, and all perfect, that is, perfect in every respect. He is Divinity, Substantiality, Truth, Symmetry, the Good. I do not mean that these are to be taken separately but that they are conceived to form a complete unity.[85] God is the Good because, as the cause of all good, he brings good to all things according to His power. He is Beauty because natural perfection is complete and harmonious. He is Truth because He is the source of all truth as the sun is of all light. He is the Father because He is the author of all things, and He guides the celestial intelligence and the world soul[86] to Himself and His thoughts. In accordance with His will He has filled all things with Himself, quickening the world soul and turning it towards Himself since He is the source of its intelligence. It is this intelligence which, after being set in order by the Father, orders the whole of nature in this world. God is ineffable and apprehensible by mind alone, as has been said, because He is neither genus nor species nor specific difference. We cannot predicate of Him evil (for it is unholy to utter such a thing) or good (for in this case He would have to participate in something else, namely goodness). Nor does He experience anything indifferent (for this is not in harmony with our notion of Him). We cannot predicate of God qualities since His perfection is not the result of having received qualities, nor can we say He lacks qualities since He has not been deprived of any quality

84. See above Chapter 9.
85. "but that...unity" Witt.
86. *Timaeus* 34b.

that befits Him. God is neither a part of something else nor a whole having parts; He is not the same as anything nor different from anything, for nothing can be predicated of Him which would separate Him from other things. He does not move nor is He moved. Our first notion of God will be that which results from abstracting the above mentioned attributes. This is how we form our conception of a point too, by abstracting from the sensible, thinking first of a surface, then a line and finally a point. Our second notion of God comes by analogy in the following way: the relation-ship which the sun has to sight and things seen (not being itself sight, but providing to sight the power to see, and to things seen the power to be seen[87]) is the relationship which the primal mind has towards understanding in the soul and the things understood. The primal mind is not the same thing as intelligence, but it provides it with the ability to know—and to things known the ability to be known—by shedding the light of truth upon them. The third way of conceiving God goes as follows: one contemplates first the beauty that resides in bodies and then passes on to the beauty of the soul, then to that which is found in customs and laws, then to the vast ocean of beauty,[88] after which one conceives of the Good itself, the goal of love and desire[89] appearing as a light and, as it were, shining upon the soul as it makes its ascent. To this one adds the notion of God because of His preeminence in honor. God is without parts because there existed nothing prior to Him. Parts are the elements of which a thing is composed and are prior to that of which they are parts. The plane is prior to the solid, and the line prior to the plane. Not having parts, moreover, God would be unmoved with regard to place and quality.[90] If He were altered by another, that agent would be more powerful then He; if by

87. *Republic* 508a, b.
88. *Symposium* 210a-d and Chapter 5 above.
89. "the goal of love and desire" Witt.
90. *Theaetetus* 181d, *Parmenides* 138c.

Himself, He would be altered either for the worse or for the better;[91] both hypotheses are absurd. From all of this it is obvious in any case that God is incorporeal. This can also be demonstrated from the following: If God were a body, He would be material and have a form, for every body is a composite of matter and accompanying form which resembles the ideas and participates in them in some way which is difficult to explain.[92] It is absurd to suppose that God is composed of matter and form, for then He would be neither simple nor primordial. Thus God must be incorporeal. Again, if God were a body, He would be made of matter, either fire or water or earth or air or some combination of these. But none of these is primordial. Furthermore, He would be produced later than matter if He were material. Since all of these assumptions are absurd, we must consider God incorporeal. Besides, if He were corporeal, He would be corruptible, generated and changeable, each of which is absurd in the case of God.

11

It can be shown that qualities are incorporeal. Every body is a substance; a quality, however, is not a substance but an accident. A quality, therefore, is not a body. Every quality is in a substance, but no body is in a substance. Therefore a quality is not a body. Moreover, one quality can be the opposite of another quality, but a body cannot be the opposite of another body. A body, in so far as it is a body, does not differ from another body at all; it differs because of quality and emphatically not because it is a body. Therefore qualities are not bodies. It is very reasonable too that, as matter is without qualities, qualities are without matter. But if qualities are without matter, they would also be incorporeal. Moreover, if qualities were bodies, two or three bodies would be in

91. *Republic* 381b, d.
92. *Timaeus* 50c.

the same place which is utterly absurd. If qualities are immaterial, then that which creates them must also be immaterial. Besides, active principles cannot fail to be incorporeal principles.[93] Bodies are subject to external influence, are in a state of flux, and are not always the same or in the same state. They are neither stable nor permanent. In cases in which bodies appear to produce an action, one will discover that earlier they were acted upon. Thus as there is something absolutely passive, so there must be something that is strictly active. It would be impossible to find such a thing to be other than immaterial. Such then is our treatment of first principles. It can be called a theological treatment. We must move next into what is called the realm of Physics, beginning in the following way.

12

There must exist Ideas which are specific models of the sensible objects that are found existing in nature separately, and it is of these Ideas that there is knowledge and definition. For besides all men we form the idea of man, and besides all horses, the idea of horse, and generically besides living things, the idea of a living thing that is unbegotten and immortal. Just as one seal can make many impressions and one individual thousands and thousands of likenesses, the Idea is the primordial cause which brings it about that each thing resembles the Idea itself. It must also be that the most beautiful artifact in creation, the universe, was fashioned by God as He gazed upon some Idea of the universe[94] which was the model for it and of which it is a copy. The universe was made by the Demiurge to resemble this Idea in keeping with the most marvelous providence. His reason for creating was that He is good.[95] He fashioned the

---

93. "Besides...principles" Witt.
94. *Timaeus* 28a.
95. *Timaeus* 29e.

world, therefore, from the whole of matter which had been, prior to the birth of heaven, moving chaotically and discordantly. He brought it from disorder into the most perfect order,[96] arranging its parts with numbers and shapes that were fitting, so that one can discern now the ratios of fire and earth to air and water.[97] These contained traces of their true nature and had the capacity to function as elements, but they were agitating matter and being agitated by it without reason or measure. God produced the universe using the whole of each one of the four elements, all the fire, all the earth, all the water and air that existed, leaving out no part nor power of them.[98] The Demiurge thought first of all that His creation should be corporeal and completely tangible and visible and that without fire and earth nothing could be either visible or tangible. According to the most likely line of reasoning, then, He fashioned it out of earth and fire. Then, since there was need for some link to be in the middle to bind the two together, and since the divine bond is proportion which by nature unifies itself and what it binds together, and since the universe was not flat[99] (in which case one mean would have been sufficient) but spherical, two means were required for its harmonious union.[100] For this reason air and water were placed in the middle between fire and earth, after the manner of a proportion. Thus fire is to air as air is to water and water is to earth and vice versa. Because the creator left nothing out, He made a universe that is unique, the only one generated[101] and equal in number to the Idea it imitates, which is one. Moreover, it is immune to disease and old age[102] in as much as nothing which by nature could harm it can approach it; it is self-sufficient and in need

---

96. *Timaeus* 30a.
97. Following Louis' interpretation.
98. *Timaeus* 32c.
99. *Timaeus* 32a and ff.
100. εἰς συναρμογήν "harmonious union," Witt.
101. *Timaeus* 31b, 92c.
102. *Timaeus* 33a.

of nothing from without. As far as shape is concerned, He bestowed upon it a spherical one[103] which is the most beautiful of all, the roomiest and the most mobile. And since the universe needed neither sight nor hearing nor any thing else of that sort, it was not fitted out with organs.[104] God removed all movements from it except the circular which He granted it as the movement most appropriate to intelligence and wisdom.[105]

13

The elements of which the cosmos is composed are two, body and soul. The former of these is visible and tangible, the latter invisible and intangible. Now, it happens that the power and constitution of each is different. The corporeal part of the cosmos has come to be from fire, earth, water and air.[106] Taking these four which did not yet have the status of elements,[107] the Demiurge of the cosmos gave them the shape of a pyramid, a cube, an octahedron, an icosahedron and, above all, a dodecahedron. When matter took the form of a pyramid, it became fire, this form being the most pointed and slender[108] and made of the least number of triangles. As far as matter took the form of the octahedron, it assumed the qualities of air; to the extent that it took on the form of the icosahedron, it had the qualities of water. The Demiurge gave to earth the form of the cube. Earth is therefore the most solid and the most stable.[109] He used the form of the dodecahedron for the whole. More fundamental than all of these is the plane,[110] for planes are

---

103. *Timaeus* 33b.
104. *Timaeus* 33c.
105. *Timaeus* 34a.
106. *Timaeus* 32c.
107. *Timaeus* 30a and 53b.
108. "the most pointed and slender" Witt; *Timaeus* 56a, b.
109. *Timaeus* 55e.
110. *Timaeus* 53c.

prior to solids. Two triangles are the ancestors, as it were, of the plane, namely the two most beautiful right triangles, the scalene and the isosceles. The scalene has one right angle, one two-thirds of a right angle and the other a third of a right angle.[111] The first triangle, I mean the scalene, is the constitutive element of the pyramid, the octahedron and icosahedron. The pyramid is composed of four equilateral triangles each of which is divided into six scalene triangles which have already been described.[112] The octahedron is likewise formed of eight triangles, each of which is divided into six scalene triangles, and the icosahedron of twenty triangles.[113] The other triangle, the isosceles, is the constitutive element of the cube, for four isosceles triangles coming together form a square, and the cube consists of six of these squares. For the whole God used the dodecahedron,[114] wherefore twelve constellations can be seen in the sky in the circle of the Zodiac and each of them is divided into thirty parts. Similarly, in the dodecahedron each of the twelve pentagons is divided into five triangles so that each of them consists of six triangles. In the dodecahedron we find a total of 360 triangles, which happens to be the same number as the degrees of the Zodiac. Matter, then, after being shaped by the deity into these forms, was moving about at first without any order. It was then reduced to order by God, all things being put into harmony and balance with one another.[115] These elements do not remain at rest, but move incessantly, and they impart this motion to matter.[116] Because the elements are caught up in the rotation of the world, they are driven around with it, and, striking against one another, the lighter elements are carried into the places which the more compact had occupied. This is why no vacuum is left, no place

111. *Timaeus* 53d.
112. *Timaeus* 54d, e.
113. *Timaeus* 55a, b.
114. *Timaeus* 55c.
115. *Timaeus* 30a, 53a, 69b.
116. *Timaeus* 52e-53a.

devoid of body,[117] and since the irregular motion persists, it gives rise to agitation.[118] Matter is shaken by the elements, and they by it.[119]

14

Having established the composition of bodies, Plato uses the powers that are evident in the soul to instruct us about it. For since we judge all things with the soul, God has quite reasonably placed the principles of all that is in it in order that, as we see all objects which come to our attention through kinship and likeness, we may posit the soul's reality in harmony with the observed facts.[120] While asserting then that there exists an intelligible reality which is indivisible, Plato has also posited the existence of another which is divisible and relates to bodies. Thus he reveals that the soul is able to apprehend either of these with its thought. Seeing identity and difference in both the sphere of the intelligible and that of the divisible, He [the Demiurge] made the soul with contributions from all of these. [121] For either like is recognized by like, as the Pythagoreans are fond of saying, or the dissimilar is recognized by the dissimilar, as Heraclitus the physical philosopher used to say. Now, when Plato says that the world was created,[122] we must not understand him to mean that there was once a time in which there was no world, but that it is always in a state of coming-to-be[123] and reveals a cause which is more primordial than itself. And God did not make the world soul, which is eternal, but He brings order to it. He could be said to make it in this sense only that by arousing it

117. *Timaeus* 58a, b.
118. *Timaeus* 58c.
119. *Timaeus* 52e.
120. "We may posit...facts," Witt. The text is corrupt at the beginning of this chapter. Some editors suspect a lacuna; I have followed Louis.
121. *Timaeus* 37c.
122. *Timaeus* 28b.
123. ἀεὶ ἐν γενέσει ἐστὶ, "it is always in a state of coming-to-be," Dillon; *Timaeus* 38c.

from, as it were, lethargy and a deep sleep, and turning its mind and itself towards Himself in order that it may gaze upon the intelligibles, it receives the Ideas and Forms as it strives after His thoughts. It is obvious then that the world is living and intelligent,[124] for God wanted to make the best world, and consequently He endowed it with both life and intelligence. Creation endowed with a soul is, all things considered, superior to creation that lacks soul, and the intelligent and intelligence cannot in all likelihood exist without soul. Since the soul extends from the center to the extremities of the cosmos,[125] it came about that the soul surrounded its body in a circle and completely enveloped it. The result of this is that the soul stretches around the world and in this way binds and holds it together. Its exterior parts, to be sure, are preeminent over its interior parts,[126] for the exterior world soul remains undivided while that which is within is divided into seven circles, distributed from the beginning according to double and triple intervals.[127] The part enveloped by the sphere that remains undivided resembles the Same while the divided part resembles the Different.[128] Since the movement of heaven which surrounds all is regular, it is uniform and orderly; that of the interior parts, however, is varied and variable with its risings and settings and is therefore called 'wandering.'[129] The exterior part of the world soul is borne to the right since it moves from the east to the west.[130] The interior part moves contrariwise, that is to the left, coming to meet the cosmos from west to east. God made both the stars and the planets. The stars are fixed; they are ornaments of the sky and the night, and their number is very great. The planets are seven in number; they exist to generate number

---

124. *Timaeus* 30b, c.
125. *Timaeus* 34b, 36e.
126. *Timaeus* 36c.
127. *Timaeus* 36d.
128. *Timaeus* 36c.
129. *Timaeus* 38c.
130. *Timaeus* 36c.

and time,[131] and to reveal that which is. God made time to be the interval of the movement of the universe, an image, as it were, of eternity which measures the stability of the eternal world.[132] The wandering stars are not all the same in power.[133] The sun is the leader of all, revealing and making manifest all things. The moon is considered second in rank because of its power, and the other planets are ranked analogously, each according to its destiny. The moon determines the length of the month, taking that much time to complete its orbit and catch up with the sun. The sun determines the length of the year for, by completing the circle of the Zodiac in that time, it brings to fulfillment the seasons of the year. The other planets have each its own proper period of revolution which are not visible to ordinary people but only to the educated. All these revolutions work together to bring about the perfect number and the perfect time when all the planets come to the same point and form a pattern such that, if one imagines a straight line drawn perpendicularly from the fixed sphere to the earth, the centers of all can be seen on this line. Since there are seven spheres in the planetary sphere, God fashioned seven visible bodies out of a substance which is like fire, and He fixed them to the spheres that come from the wandering circle of the Different. He placed the moon in the first orbit next to the earth; the sun he assigned to the second orbit. The morning star, Venus, and the one called 'the sacred star of Hermes [Mercury] He assigned to the orbit that moves with the same speed as the sun, but is farther away. He placed the other planets on a higher plane, each in its proper sphere. The slowest of them, which some people call the star of Kronos [Saturn], lies just below the sphere of the fixed stars; the second slowest, Zeus' star [Jupiter], comes after it, and next, Ares' star

131. *Timaeus* 37d-38c, 38e.

132. "to be...of the universe." Witt; *Timaeus* 37d.

133. Albinus' discussion of the orbits of the planets follows *Timaeus* 38c-40a although Plato only mentions four 'planets,' the moon, the sun, Venus and Mercury.

[Mars]; eighth is the supreme power which envelopes all the others. All of these are living beings endowed with intelligence; they are gods and they are spherical in shape.

15

There are also other divine spirits[134] which one could call 'created gods'.[135] They exist in each of the elements. Some are visible, others invisible, and they are found in ether, fire, air and water so that no part of the cosmos is without soul or life superior to mortal nature.[136] All sublunar and terrestrial things are subject to these divinities. Now God Himself is the maker of everything, both of gods and lesser divinities and, thanks to His will, the whole will not experience dissolution.[137] His children guide all other things,[138] and they do whatever they do in accordance with His command and His example. From them come presages, ominous signs, dreams, oracles and whatever else is devised by mortals in practicing divination.[139] The earth lies in the middle of the universe, held fast about the axis which runs through the All.[140] It is the guardian of day and night and is the most ancient of the gods in heaven, being born just after the world soul. It provides us with nourishment in abundance, and around it the *kosmos* revolves. The earth is a star, but one that is at rest, because it lies in equilibrium at the center of the *kosmos* like those that revolve about it. Ether is found in the outermost area which is divided into the sphere of the fixed stars and that of the planets. After these is the sphere of air, and in the midst of it is the earth with its own moisture.

134. δαίμονες.
135. *Timaeus* 40d.
136. *Timaeus* 30e, d and 31a, b.
137. *Timaeus* 41b.
138. *Timaeus* 41a.
139. *Timaeus* 71.
140. *Timaeus* 40b, c.

16

When all things had been put in order by God, He still had left three types of mortal creatures which were destined to be, namely the winged, the aquatic and those that go on foot.[141] He enjoined the creation of these to the young gods lest they be immortal because they were fashioned by Him.[142] They then created the mortal species after borrowing from primordial matter for specific periods of time certain portions which are to be repaid to it again.[143] Now since the Father of all and the young gods were concerned about the human race as most akin to the gods, the Creator of the universe sent down to the earth the souls of this species, equal in number to the stars.[144] He then placed each soul in its kindred star as in a vehicle, and in order that He would be blameless, He explained to them all the laws of destiny as a lawgiver would. He told them that the feelings which arise from the body would be those character-istic of mortals, first sensations, then pleasure and pain, and fear and anger; that souls which master these feelings and are by no means overpowered by them will live just lives and will return to the star related to them.[145] Those souls dominated by injustice, on the other hand, will return at their second birth to live a woman's life, and if they do not cease their unjust ways, they will be transformed finally into wild beasts. There is to be no end to their sufferings until they conquer the vices that have become attached to them and return to their proper state.[146]

17

As their initial act the gods fashioned man out of earth, fire, air

141. *Timaeus* 41a, b.
142. *Timaeus* 41c.
143. *Timaeus* 42e-43a.
144. *Timaeus* 41d.
145. *Timaeus* 42a, b.
146. *Timaeus* 42c, d, e.

and water,[147] borrowing certain portions to be repaid later.[148] Putting them together with invisible bolts, they fashioned a unified body. Then they attached to the head the principal part of the soul which had been sent down, giving it the brain to be its "field of labor," as it were.[149] About the face they placed the organs of sensation so that each would perform the function appropriate to it.[150] They synthesized the marrow out of the smooth, regular triangles from which the elements were made; its purpose is to produce semen.[151] Bones they made of earth and marrow moistened and frequently dipped into water and fire.[152] Sinews were made of bone and flesh, and flesh itself of a kind of fermented mixture that was salty and acrid.[153] They placed bone around the marrow and around the bones sinews to join them together. By means of sinews the joints bend and are bound together. Thanks to the flesh, the bones have a cover over them,[154] in some places white, in others a dark color,[155] for the greater good of the body. From these same elements were formed the viscera, that is the abdomen, the entrails which coil about it, the windpipe which comes down from the mouth and the pharynx. The former goes to the stomach, the latter to the lungs. Food is digested in the stomach after being broken down into particles and softened by the heat of the breath.[156] Thus it passes to the whole body ready to be assimilated into the system.[157] Two veins run along the spine until they twine round the head from opposite directions, and they divide at that point into

147. *Timaeus* 42e.
148. *Timaeus* 43a.
149. ἄρουραν, champ de labour, Louis; *Timaeus* 73c, d.
150. *Timaeus* 45a, b.
151. *Timaeus* 73b, c.
152. *Timaeus* 73e.
153. *Timaeus* 74d.
154. *ibid.*
155. Following Louis' text; "thin and in another place more abundant" Witt.
156. *Timaeus* 79a, b.
157. κατὰ τὰς οἰκείας μεταβολάς, "ready to be assimilated into the system," Witt; sous la forme que chacun a reçue, Louis.

many branches.[158] After the gods made man and bound to his body the soul to be its mistress, for good reasons they placed the ruling part of the soul in the head where are located the sources of marrow and sinews[159] and where the mental problems that are caused by the emotions arise. The senses surround the head as if they were bodyguards protecting the ruling power. In this place also are lodged reason, judgment and contemplation. They placed the passionate part of the soul lower down, the irascible around the heart and concupiscible in the lower abdomen around the navel. We shall speak about these later.[160]

18

After having placed on the face the light-giving eyes, the gods enclosed in them the luminous portion of fire[161] which, because it is subtle and continuous, they considered akin to daylight. This flows out through the whole of the eyes most easily, but especially through the center of them, thanks to its unmixed purity. Being sympathetic to the external light, as like is to like, it produces the sense of sight.[162] Hence at night when daylight has departed or is obscured, the flow of light from us no longer encounters the ambient air but is held within where it calms and disperses our inner movements and brings on sleep. Because of this the eyelids close. If the repose is profound,[163] an almost dreamless sleep ensues. If, on the other hand, some movements remain, numerous images appear to us. Both images that arise directly while we are awake and while we are asleep are formed thus. Besides these there are also images in mirrors and other surfaces which are shiny and smooth. These

158. *Timaeus* 77d, e.
159. *Timaeus* 73d, e.
160. Chapter 24.
161. *Timaeus* 45b, c.
162. *Timaeus* 45d.
163. *Timaeus* 45e-46a.

have no other cause but reflection and vary to the extent that the surface is convex, concave or turned lengthwise.[164] The images will differ as the rays are reflected in different directions. A convex surface disperses them while a concave one draws them together.[165] Thus in some mirrors left and right appear reversed, in others they are correctly placed and in still others the top and bottom are reversed.

19

Hearing was created for the perception of sound. Beginning with movement about the head, it ends in the seat of the liver.[166] Sound is the stroke transmitted through the ears, brain and blood which penetrates all the way to the soul. It is shrill when the movement is rapid and deep when it is slow. It is loud when there is much movement, soft when there is little. Next, in the nostrils there is the faculty for perceiving odors.[167] Smell is the sensation that descends from the veins in the nostrils to the regions around the navel. The various species of smells have not been named except for two large classes, good and bad, which are also designated pleasant and painful.[168] Every odor is denser than air and more subtle than water. The proof of this is that the things to which some type of smell is attributed have not yet undergone a complete transformation, but they have a share of water and of air.[169] These are things such as smoke and mist, for it is as these things are being transformed into each other that the sensation of smell occurs. The gods provided us with taste to be the judge of the most varied flavors. They have run veins from the tongue to the heart[170] which are designed to test and

164. *Timaeus* 46c.
165. *Timaeus* 46b, c.
166. *Timaeus* 67b.
167. *Timaeus* 66d.
168. *Timaeus* 67a.
169. *Timaeus* 66e.
170. *Timaeus* 64c, d.

judge flavors. These veins contract and expand as juices come in contact with them, and they discern the differences in flavors. There are seven different flavors: sweet, acid, astringent, harsh, salty, pungent and bitter.[171] Now it happens that among these flavors the sweet has a property that is different from all the others; it very conveniently spreads moisture all around the tongue. As for the others, some such as acids disturb and rend the tongue while others that are pungent inflame it and rise upward.[172] Bitter tastes have a strong detergent power so as to even cause the tongue to waste away. Salty savors gently cleanse and purge the tongue.[173] Among those that contract and close the pores, some are rougher, namely the astringent, while others do this less so, namely the harsh savors.[174] The sense of touch has been provided by the gods to perceive the hot and the cold, the hard and the soft, the light and the heavy, the smooth and the rough, and to judge the differences between them.[175] We call things that are receptive to touch resilient; those that do not yield we call resistant.[176] Now this depends upon the bases of the bodies themselves, for those that have large bases are solid and firm while those that rest on a small base yield easily, are soft and easy to move. A rough body unites unevenness with hardness; a smooth body combines regularity and density.[177] The experience of 'hot' and the experience of 'cold' have completely opposite causes.[178] The one cuts through a body with its sharpness and roughness and produces the sensation of heat; the other, which causes cold, consists of coarser particles, and, as they enter, they push out the smaller particles and struggle to enter their places. A

---

171. *Timaeus* 65d-66c.

172. "fly upwards because of their lightness towards the senses of the head..." *Timaeus* 66a translation by Bury (Loeb).

173. *Timaeus* 65e.

174. *Timaeus* 65d.

175. *Timaeus* 61d-62d.

176. *Timaeus* 62c.

177. *Timaeus* 63e-64a.

178. *Timaeus* 62e-63a.

kind of trembling and shivering then arises, and the ensuing feeling in the body is that of being cold.[179]

20

It is incorrect to define the heavy and the light with the notions of 'up' and 'down' since 'up' and 'down' do not really exist.[180] Because the whole of heaven is spherical and uniformly finished on its exterior surface, it is wrong to speak of 'up' and 'down.' That which is drawn only with difficulty to a place other than the one it naturally occupies is heavy and that which is easily drawn is light. In addition, that which is composed of many parts is heavy; that composed of few parts is light.

21

We breathe in the following way:[181] A great quantity of air surrounds us on the outside. This air enters the body through the mouth, the nostrils and other openings which reason has made known. After being warmed, it rushes outwards toward the air that is cognate with it. An amount of outside air equal to the amount that exited from the body rushes in, and thus, as the cycle is completed unceasingly, inhalation and exhalation occur.

22

The causes of diseases are many. First of all, there may be a lack or an excess of the elements, or they may have moved to places that are not appropriate to them.[182] Secondly, the generation of homo-

179. *Timaeus* 62.
180. *Timaeus* 62e-63e.
181. *Timaeus* 79d, e.
182. *Timaeus* 82a, b.

geneous substances may have been reversed, for example, if blood
or bile or phlegm is produced from flesh.[183] All of these things are
nothing but examples of decomposition.[184] Phlegm comes from the
dissolution of new flesh.[185] Sweat and tears are, as it were, the watery
part or serum of phlegm.[186] When phlegm is left over on the exterior, it produces skin diseases and leprosy;[187] when it is mixed in
the interior of the body with black bile, it causes epilepsy, the so-
called 'sacred disease.' Phlegm that is acrid and salty is the cause of
rheumatic diseases.[188] All parts that are inflamed suffer these af-
flictions because of bile.[189] In fact thousands of different diseases are
the work of bile and phlegm. The continuous fever comes from an
excess of fire, the quotidean fever from an excess of air, the tertian
from that of water and the quartan from that of earth.

23

Next we must speak of the soul, picking up treatment of it at this
point at the risk of appearing to repeat ourselves. After receiving
from the primal God the human soul, which is immortal, as we will
show,[190] the gods charged with fashioning the mortal species joined
to it two mortal parts. But lest the divine and immortal part of the
soul be infected with mortal nonsense, they placed it at the top of
the body, on the acropolis, so to speak,[191] and they declared it the
ruler and king, and they assigned to it a residence, namely the head,
which has a form similar to that of the universe. They then placed

183. *Timaeus* 82c, d.
184. σύντηξις, decomposition, Witt; dissolution, Louis; colliquescence, L.S.J.
185. *Timaeus* 83b.
186. *Timaeus* 83d, e.
187. *Timaeus* 85a.
188. τῶν ἐν ῥύσει παθῶν, defluxionary affections, Witt; affections catarrheuses, Louis;
Cf. *Timaeus* 85b.
189. *Timaeus* 85b.
190. See Chapters 14, 17 and 25.
191. *Timaeus* 69a-70b; *Republic* 560b.

under it the rest of the body as a servant and as a vehicle,[192] and they assigned one dwelling place to one mortal part of the soul and another to the other.[193] They placed the irascible element in the heart; the concupiscible part they located in the area between the boundary at the navel and the diaphram,[194] tethering it there as if it were a mad and untamed beast. They made the lungs soft, bloodless and porous like a sponge for the sake of the heart so that when pounding with emotion it would have some padding. The liver is to arouse the appetitive part of the soul and to pacify it, having as it does a capacity for both sweetness and bitterness. It can also reveal prophetic signs by means of dreams. Because the liver is smooth, compact and shiny, there is reflected in it the power of thought that comes from the mind.[195] The spleen was made for the sake of the liver, to cleanse it and render it shiny; it receives at any rate the impurities that collect around the liver after certain diseases.

24

We will next learn that the soul is tripartite, corresponding to its faculties, and that its parts have been assigned to their places according to reason. First of all, things which are separated by nature are different.[196] The faculty of suffering and the reasoning faculty are naturally separated if, at any rate, the latter concerns itself with the intelligibles and the former with pain and pleasure. Furthermore, the faculty of suffering is found in all living things.[197] Now, since the faculty of suffering and that of reasoning are by nature different, they must be separated as to location for they are

---

192. *Timaeus* 44d, e.
193. *Timaeus* 69e.
194. *Timaeus* 70d, e.
195. δύναμις, "power of thought," Bury in Loeb *Timaeus* 71b.
196. *Republic* 436-437a; *Timaeus* 89d-90d.
197. *Republic* 441b.

found to clash with one another, and nothing can be at war with itself. Nor can things opposed to one another be in the same place at the same time. One can see in the case of Medea anger struggling against reason, for she says,

> What wickedness I mean to do, alas, I know—
> But my good resolutions rage doth overthrow.[198]

Also in the case of Laius who carried off Chrysippus we see desire at war with reason, for he says,

> Ah, 'tis an evil that doth seem divine, for men
> To see the good, and not to act upon it then.[199]

A further proof that the rational is different from the passionate comes from the fact that each must be cultivated in its own way, the rational through education,[200] the passionate through the development of good habits.[201]

25

The immortality of the soul Plato proves in the following way: To whatever the soul is attached it brings life as one of its natural qualities. But that which brings life to a thing does not admit of death itself. Such a thing is immortal,[202] and if it is immortal, it is also indestructible.[203] The soul is an incorporeal substance, immutable in its essence, intelligible, invisible and simple.[204] It is there-

198. Euripides' *Medea*, 1078-1079, Witt's translation.
199. Euripides' *Chrysippus*, Witt's translation.
200. *Republic* 493b.
201. *Republic* 518e.
202. Cf. *Phaedo* 105c, d, e.
203. *Phaedo* 106a-d.
204. *Phaedo* 79b-81c.

fore uncompounded,[205] indissoluble[206] and indivisible. The body is the exact opposite; it is sensible,[207] visible, divisible,[208] composite[209] and of diverse kinds.[210] And in fact when the soul draws near to the sensible through the mediation of the body, it becomes dizzy and is troubled and, as it were, drunk.[211] *Vis-a-vis* the intelligible world, however, it remains within itself, composed and tranquil.[212] But if the soul is troubled when near an object, it is because it has no resemblance to that object.[213] Rather as a result it resembles the intelligible, and the intelligible is indivisible and indestructible. Moreover, the soul by nature rules,[214] but that which by nature rules is like unto the divine. Thus the soul, since it resembles the divine, would be indestructible and incorruptible. Things which are direct opposites[215] and exist not *per se* but accidently are by nature produced from one another. What men call life is the opposite of death. Therefore, in as much as death is the separation of the soul from the body, life is a union of a body and a soul, the latter of which, it is clear, existed previously. If the soul will exist after death and it existed before it fell in with a body, then it is very easy to believe that the soul is eternal, for we cannot imagine anything that would destroy it. Again, if learning is recollection, the soul would be immortal.[216] That learning is recollection we may be convinced in the following way: Learning could not come about except through recollection of things learned long ago.[217] For, if we form

205. *Phaedo* 78c.
206. *Phaedo* 80b.
207. *Phaedo* 83b.
208. *Timaeus* 37a.
209. *Phaedo* 78b.
210. *Phaedo* 80b.
211. *Phaedo* 79c.
212. *Phaedo* 79d.
213. *Phaedo* 79e.
214. *Phaedo* 80a.
215. *Phaedo* 70c-72e.
216. *Phaedo* 72e and ff.
217. *Phaedo* 74a-75d.

concepts of universals from particulars, how could we examine all
the particulars, since they are infinite in number, or how could we
form concepts from a few instances? We could be deceived thinking, for example, that only that which breathes is an animal. Or how
could concepts function as principles? We form concepts then
from certain slight flickers of recollection.[218] We are reminded by
a few particulars which happened to come to our attention of things
we knew long ago but forgot when we entered our bodies. Again,
the soul is not corrupted by its own wickedness,[219] nor could it be
corrupted by the wickedness of another, nor in fact by anything
else; hence it would be indestructible.[220] Now that which is self-
moved from the beginning is eternally in motion, and such a thing
is immortal. The soul is self-moved,[221] and that which is self-moved
is the first principle of motion and generation. But a first principle
is without beginning and is indestructible. Such would be the soul
of the universe and such would be also the human soul since both
share the same mixture. Plato says that the soul is self-moved[222]
because life is innate to it and it is eternally in action of its own
accord. According to Plato, one can affirm, therefore, that rational
souls are immortal. But whether souls lacking reason are immortal
is contested. It is probable that non-rational souls, being driven by
mere images and making use of neither reasoning nor judgment
and lacking the conclusions that follow from speculation, universal
distinctions and all understanding of the intellectual, are not of the
same essence as rational souls and are, therefore, mortal and
destructible. It follows logically from this thesis that souls are
immortal, that they enter into different bodies and follow the
natural development of the embryo in each case. Souls pass through
many bodies, both human and non-human, abiding by their

218. μικρῶν αἰθυγμάτων (small sparks) "certain slight flickers of recollection" Witt.
219. *Republic* 609c, d.
220. *Republic* 610b, c.
221. *Phaedrus* 245c, d.
222. *Phaedrus* 245e.

numbers[223] either because of the the will of the gods or because of their own intemperance and love of the body. The body and the soul are related to one another, one might say, as are fire and asphalt.[224] The souls of the gods possess discernment[225] (which one could also call the cognitive faculty), the impulsive faculty (which could be called exhortative) and the appropriative. These faculties exist also in human souls, but as a result of being embodied they undergo a change, as it were, the appropriative into the appetitive and the impulsive into the irrascible.[226]

26

Concerning fate Plato's teaching goes something like this:[227] All things lie within the realm of fate, he says, but all things are not fated. For fate, while having the status of law, does not say, for example, that this person will do this and that person will suffer that. This would go on to infinity since the number of individuals is infinite and so is the number of things that happen to them. Also, what is in our power would disappear as well as praise and blame and everything similar. What fate does decree is that, because this soul chooses such and such a life and performs such and such acts, these results follow for it. The soul is thus autonomous, and to act or not act lies within its power.[228] It has not been coerced to do this or that, but the consequences of its actions will come about in accordance with fate. For example, if Paris carries off Helen, it being within his power to do so, it will follow that the Greeks will

---

223. "abiding...numbers" Witt. Cf. *Timaeus* 92c.
224. "Cette comparaison ne se trouve pas chez Platon." Louis.
225. *Politicus* 260b.
226. *Republic* IV.
227. "No one dialogue sets forth Plato's teaching about fate, but the ideas which Albinus expresses here reflect a number of passages from the dialogues, e.g. *Phaedrus* 255b, *Republic* 566a, 617d, *Protagoras* 320d, 321c, *Phaedo* 115a, *Laws* 873c, 904c." Louis.
228. *Republic* 617d, e.

go to war for her. So also did Apollo foretell to Laius:

> If thou beget a son, by him thou shalt be slain.[229]

Laius and his begetting of a son are encompassed by the oracle, but only the consequence is fated. The possible by its nature somehow falls between truth and falsity. That which lies within our power is born, as it were, on the possible which is by nature indeterminate. Whatever happens as a result of our choice will be either true or false. What is in potency differs from an existing state and from what exists in actuality. For what is in potency reveals a certain aptitude for things which have not yet become a state. Thus a boy will be said to be a potential grammarian, flute player or carpenter; he will be in the state of being one or two of these at that moment when he has learned and possesses some of the requisite habits. He will possess them in actuality whenever he acts according to that habit he has acquired. But the possible is none of these; it is indeterminate and it acquires the character of truth or falsity depending upon which way we by our own free will choose.

27

Next let us speak briefly about Plato's ethical teaching. He thought that the Good that is greatest and most honorable was difficult to find and,[230] once found, he thought it unsafe to communicate it to everybody. At any rate, he shared his lectures on the Good with only a very few of his friends who had been carefully chosen. If, however, one examines Plato's writings carefully, he will find that the good for us has been located in the knowledge and contemplation of the primal Good which one could also call God

---

229. Euripides, *Phoenician Women*, 19, Witt's translation.
230. "Albinus semble faire allusion specialement au livre VI de *la Republique*, 506 et sqq." Louis.

or the First Intelligence. For Plato thought that all things considered good by men in any way whatever acquired that name because they participated in some way or other in that primal and most honorable Good[231] in the same way that sweet and hot things are so called because of their participation in their primaries. Of our possessions intellect and reason alone arrive at a likeness to the Good.[232] Because of this the good for us is beautiful, holy, god-like, lovely, symmetrical[233] and marvelous. Of the things called good by the masses such as health, beauty, strength, wealth[234] and the like, not one is altogether good unless it happens to be used as a result of virtue. Separated from virtue, they have merely the status of matter, becoming evil in the hands of those who use them wickedly.[235] Sometimes Plato calls these 'mortal goods.' Plato thought that happiness was to be found not in human goods but in divine and blessed ones. Hence he used to say that truly philosophical souls are full of great and marvelous goods, and after their separation from the body they become companions of the gods and make the rounds with them,[236] contemplating the Plain of Truth[237] since even in this life they longed for knowledge of the Good, and they honored the pursuit of it above all else. From this pursuit the eye of their soul—an 'eye' more worth saving than a thousand bodily eyes—is cleansed and purified, so to speak, after having been ruined and blinded.[238] Because of this, philosophical souls become capable of reaching the nature of all that is rational. Plato likens senseless men to those who dwell beneath the earth and have never seen a bright light. They see only dim shadows of terrestrial bodies

---

231. *Phaedo* 100c, d.
232. *Republic* 508c.
233. *Timaeus* 87d.
234. *Laws* 631b and 661a.
235. *Laws* 661b, c.
236. *Phaedrus* 248a.
237. *Phaedrus* 248b.
238. *Republic* 527c.

and think they are clearly perceiving realities. Thus, after they have found a road up from the darkness and have advanced towards pure light, they quite reasonably condemn what appeared true to them earlier, and they especially condemn themselves for having been deceived. So also those who move on from the darkness of life to things truly divine and beautiful despise what they previously marveled at, and they have a stronger desire to contemplate the divine. Of them it seems correct to say that beauty itself is the only good and that virtue suffices for happiness.[239] Why the Good and why moral beauty consist of knowledge of the first cause is something Plato made clear through the whole of his writings, and he states in the first book of the *Laws* that other things are good by participation therein.[240] "There exist two types of goods, human goods and divine ones," and so forth.[241] But if something is separated from the essence of the Supreme Good[242] and has no share in it, even though unthinking men call it good, it will be, according to Plato in the *Euthydemus*, an even greater evil.[243] Plato's belief that the virtues are to be chosen for their own sake should be seen as a consequence of his belief that the beautiful[244] is the only good. This has been set forth by Plato in a great many of his dialogues but especially in the *Republic*. He considers the person who has the aforementioned knowledge to be most fortunate and most happy. This is not because of the honors he will receive because he is as he is nor because of other rewards, but even if he is unknown to all men and even if so-called evils such as loss of civil rights and exile and death come to him, he will be happy. On the other hand, the person who lacks this knowledge but possesses all of what are deemed goods, such as wealth, absolute royal power, health and strength of

---

239. *Gorgias* 474c.
240. "that...therein." Witt.
241. 631b.
242. τοῦ πρώτου τῆς οὐσίας, "the essence of the Supreme Good." Witt.
243. 281d.
244. τὸ καλόν, "moral beauty" Witt.

body and beauty, will not be any happier at all.

28

As a consequence of all of this, Plato posited 'assimilation to God, as far as one is able,'[245] as the goal. He deals with this in a number of ways. Sometimes, as in the *Theaetetus*,[246] he says that assimilation to God is to be prudent, just and holy: "therefore we ought to try to escape from earth to the dwelling of the gods as quickly as we can."[247] "To escape is to become like God, so far as this is possible; and to become like God is to become righteous and holy and wise."[248] Sometimes, as in the last book of the *Republic*, he says that to be just alone is to be like God: "...for the gods never neglect a man who is eagerly wanting to be just and to become as like a god as it is possible for a man to be by practicing virtue."[249] In the *Phaedo* he states that assimilation to God means to become temperate and just, using words something like these: "...they are the happiest and likely to go to the best place, who have aimed at 'popular' or 'civic' virtue, at what they call temperance and justice..."[250] Sometimes he says the goal is to be assimilated to God; at other times he says it is to follow Him, as when he states: "...according to the ancient story, there is a god who holds in his hands the beginning and the end..." and so forth.[251] Sometimes he asserts both, as when he says "that [soul] which best follows a god and becomes most like thereunto..." and so forth.[252] For the good is the beginning of benefit[253] and it is said to be from God. The end, to be assimilated to God, would

245. *Theaetetus* 176b.
246. *Theaetetus* 176a, b.
247. *Theaetetus* 176a, Fowler.
248. *Theaetetus* 176a, Fowler.
249. *Republic* 613a, Grube.
250. *Phaedo* 82a, b, Bluck.
251. *Laws* 715e, Saunders.
252. *Phaedrus* 248a, Hackforth.
253. ὠφελείας ἀρχή, "beginning of benefit," Witt.

therefore follow upon the beginning. By 'God' it obviously means
the one who is in heaven, not, by Zeus, the one who is above it, the
one who does not have virtue but transcends it. Hence one could
rightly say that misery is the evil-doing of one's *daimon* and happiness is a good disposition of it. We may succeed in becoming like
unto God if we have suitable natural abilities, good habits and
education and discipline in accordance with the law, and most
important of all, by using reason, education and teachings that have
been handed down.[254] Thus we shall rise above human concerns for
the most part and always be devoted to intelligible realities. The
preparations for initiation and the preliminary purification of the
daimon within us,[255] if one is to be initiated into the higher sciences,
should be through music, arithmetic, astronomy and geometry.[256]
We ought at the same time take care of the body through gymnastics,
which renders it fit for both war and peace.[257]

29

Granted that virtue is something divine, in itself it is a perfect and
supremely excellent state of the soul. It renders a person gracious,
consistent and steadfast in speaking and acting in relation to one's
self and to others. The notion of virtue includes rational virtues and
those that pertain to the irrational part of the soul, such as courage
and temperance. Courage pertains to the spirited part and temperance to the appetitive. For since the rational, the spirited and
appetitive are different, different too would be the perfection of
each. The perfection of the rational part of the soul is wisdom, that
of the spirited is courage and that of the appetitive is temperance.
Wisdom is knowledge of what is good, of what is evil and what is

---

254. *Laws* 803a.
255. *Phaedo* 107d.
256. *Republic* VII.
257. *Republic* 403c and ff.

neither. Temperance consists in the proper ordering of desires and passions[258] and in bringing them to obedience of the ruling authority, that is reason.[259] Now when we say that temperance is proper ordering and obedience, we mean something like this: it is a power under which our desires can become well ordered and docile towards their natural leader, reason. Courage consists in preserving a legitimate idea about what is to be feared and what is not,[260] that is a power to keep safe legitimate opinions. Justice is a harmony, so to speak, of these three virtues, wisdom, courage and temperance with one another.[261] It is the power whereby the three parts of the soul agree and come into concord one with another, and each is inclined to do what is fitting and proper for it. Thus justice may be the supreme perfection of the three virtues. When reason rules and the other parts of the soul are held in check by reason, each according to its own peculiar nature, one ought to think that then the virtues will result. Since courage preserves legitimate beliefs, it preserves right reason, for a legitimate belief is a right reason. Now right reason comes from wisdom, and in fact wisdom maintains and sustains courage. Wisdom is in effect the science of what is good. No one is able to see the Good when he is blinded by cowardice and the passions which accompany it. In the same way a person cannot be wise if he is intemperate. In general, if a person has been overcome by a passion and does something contrary to right reason, Plato says that he is the victim of ignorance and folly.[262] Thus no one could be wise who is intemperate and cowardly. Perfect virtues are, therefore, inseparable from one another.

258. *Symposium* 196c.
259. *Republic* 430e.
260. *Republic* 429b, c and 433c, d.
261. *Republic* 443d, e.
262. Louis cites *Protagoras* 345d and 357d, e; *Gorgias* 509e; *Timaeus* 86d, e and *Republic* 351a.

30

We also use the term virtue in another sense to refer to 'good natural endowments' and 'progress' towards virtue; these have the same name as the perfect virtues because of their similarity to them. Thus we call soldiers brave, and we sometimes say certain people are brave although they are fools. In these cases we are not speaking of perfect virtues. Perfect virtues obviously cannot be either increased or decreased; vices, however, admit of both increase and decrease for one person can be more foolish and more unjust than another. Vices, however, do not always accompany one another, for some are mutually exclusive and could not coexist in the same person. This is the case with foolhardiness and cowardliness and prodigality and avarice. Moreover, it is impossible that a person should exist who is afflicted with every single vice, just as it is impossible for there to be a body that possesses within itself all physical defects. We must admit then the existence of an intermediate state which is neither good nor bad, for not every person is entirely good or entirely bad. Such, for instance, are the people who are making satisfactory progress towards virtue, for it is not easy to move immediately from vice to virtue, there being a great deal of distance and opposition between the extremes. We should also consider the fact that among virtues some are of fundamental importance while others are secondary. The primary virtues are those which pertain to reason, from which the rest acquire their perfection. Secondary virtues are those which pertain to the emotive part of the soul. They perform nobly when they follow reason, not reason which is in them for they don't actually have it, but the reason granted to them by wisdom and developed by custom and discipline.[263] And, since neither knowledge nor art exists in any other part of the soul except the rational, those virtues that pertain

---

263. *Phaedo* 82b, *Republic* 619c and 518e.

to the emotions, inasmuch as they are neither arts nor sciences, are unteachable. They lack a proper object of contemplation.[264] Wisdom, however, being a science, imparts to each subordinate virtue that which is appropriate to it as the pilot points out to the sailors[265] things which they cannot see, and they obey him. The same thing could be said about a general and his soldiers. Since vices can be larger or smaller, the faults that arise from them are not all equal, but some are more serious and others less serious. Consequently some crimes are punished more severely by lawgivers than others. Although virtues are extremes because they are analogous to the straight line,[266] in another way they are means because around all of them, or at any rate most of them, can be seen two vices, one tending toward excess, the other toward deficiency. Thus, in the case of generosity, there is stinginess on one side and prodigality on the other, for there is a lack of moderation in our feelings according as we exceed what is appropriate or fall short of it. The person who does not become angry when his parents are insulted would not be considered sensible; nor would the person who is angered by everybody on every occasion be considered to have moderated his passions, but just the opposite. Again, in like manner, the person who feels no grief when his parents die is apathetic; the person who is so overwhelmed with grief as to waste away from it is excessively and immoderately sensitive. On the other hand, the person who grieves and does it reasonably has moderated his emotions. The person who fears everything and fears excessively is a coward; he who fears nothing is foolhardy while the courageous person stands in the middle. The same can be said about the other virtues. Since, therefore, moderation is the best policy with regard to the emotions, and moderation is nothing but the mean between excess and

264. οὐδὲ γὰρ ἴδιον θεώρημα ἔχουσιν, "they have no theoretic principles of their own..." Witt.

265. *Phaedrus* 247c, *Republic* 341c.

266. "analogous...line" Dillon p. 301.

deficiency, the virtues we are speaking of are means because they bring us into a mean state with respect to our emotions.[267]

31

If there is anything that lies within our power and knows no master, such must be virtue, for righteousness would not be praiseworthy if it were a matter of nature or divine dispensation. Virtue must, therefore, be voluntary, coming to be as a result of some impulse that is ardent, noble and enduring. From the fact that virtue is voluntary, it follows that vice is involuntary. For who would choose willingly to have in the most beautiful and most honorable part of himself the greatest of evils?[268] Now if a person turns toward vice, first of all it will not be as to vice that he directs himself but as to a good. And if someone falls in with evil, such a person must have been completely deceived, thinking, as he did, that he could obtain a greater good from a lesser evil. In this way he will involuntarily become involved with vice. It is impossible that a person would turn to vice desiring it for its own sake without either hope for some good or fear of a greater evil.[269] All of the injustices that the fool commits are, therefore, involuntary, for if injustice is involuntary, the unjust act will be *a fortiori* involuntary inasmuch as a deed itself is a greater evil than merely having the potential for evil but not actualizing it. And yet, although wrong-doing is involuntary, wrongdoers must be punished, but not all in the same way, for damages differ and the involuntariness can result from ignorance or passion. All such things can be eliminated by reason, by refined manners and by practice. So great an evil is injustice that committing an unjust act is more to be avoided than suffering one. The former is the work of an evil person; the latter,

267. *Phaedo* 113d.
268. *Protagoras* 345d, 358c; *Gorgias* 509c; *Laws* 731c.
269. Cf. *Meno* 77a-78b.

to suffer an injustice, is a misfortune of human frailty. Both are shameful, but to commit an injustice is more wicked to the extent that it is more shameful.[270] It is beneficial for the wrongdoer to pay the penalty just as it is for the sick person to entrust his body to the physician for treatment.[271] All punishment is, as it were, therapy for a soul that has gone wrong.

32

Since most virtues deal with emotions, we must next make clear what sort of thing an emotion is.[272] Now then, an emotion is an irrational movement of the soul towards good or evil.[273] The movement is described as irrational because emotions are neither judgments nor opinions but movements in the irrational parts of the soul. They occur in the passionate part of the soul, and, although they are ours, they are not under our control. They often arise in us against our will and in spite of our resistance. Sometimes too, although we know that what we are experiencing is neither painful nor pleasant nor frightening, we are nevertheless influenced by them. This would not happen if emotions were the same as judgments, for we reject judgments after we have condemned them whether rightly or wrongly. Emotion is related to good or to evil since *vis-a-vis* an indifferent thing no emotion is aroused. All emotions arise then in the face of either good or evil. If we think that a good is present, we are pleased, and if we think it is in the future, we feel desire. If we imagine a present evil, we are grieved; if it is a future evil, we are fearful. There are two simple and fundamental emotions, pleasure and pain;[274] all others are formed from these two. Fear and desire must not be counted along with

270. *Gorgias* 479a, 480b.
271. *Gorgias* 479a; *Sophist* 230b, c.
272. πάθος, "affection" Witt; "passion" Louis.
273. *Republic* 583e.
274. *Philebus* 44b.

pleasure and pain as fundamental and simple, for the person who is fearful is not completely deprived of pleasure.[275] And if one despaired of having his suffering removed or alleviated, he could not continue to live for even a short time. The fearful person is overwhelmed by pain and anguish; fear, therefore, is bound up with pain. The person who desires something, although he remains in a state of expectation toward what he hopes to attain, experiences pleasure, but since he is not completely confident nor does he have solid hopes, he experiences anxiety. Since, then, desire and fear are not fundamental emotions, it will be admitted without hesitation that none of the other emotions are either. I mean anger, regret,[276] jealousy,[277] etc. In all of these one sees pleasure and pain mixed, as it were.[278] Some emotions are 'wild'; some are 'tame.'[279] The tame ones are all those that exist naturally in the human being, those, in other words, that are necessary and appropriate. They are tame as long as there is moderation. But if they become immoderate, they become evil. Examples would be pleasure, pain, anger, pity and shame. It is appropriate to take pleasure in those things which are natural and to experience pain from their opposites. Anger is necessary for defending one's self and punishing enemies. Pity is an appropriate human feeling. Shame serves the purpose of making us retreat from what is base. The other emotions are 'wild'; they are unnatural and come from perversity or from bad habits. Examples are mockery, rejoicing at the misfortune of others[280] and being a misanthrope. These can be intense or not so intense, but they are defects whatever their state for they are always immoderate. On the subject of pleasure and pain, Plato says that these emotions were set in motion in us by nature from the very beginning,[281] and they

---

275. *Philebus* 36a,c.
276. Louis refers to *Cratylus* 420a, *Symposium* 197d, *Phaedrus* 253e and *Republic* 573a.
277. *Philebus* 47e.
278. *Philebus* 46b-47b.
279. *Republic* 486b, 589b.
280. *Philebus* 49d-50a.
281. *Republic* 583e.

continue to this day. Pain and suffering come to those who are aroused in an unnatural way; pleasure comes to those who have been restored to a natural state.[282] Plato thinks that the natural state for us is the mean between suffering and pleasure,[283] neither one nor the other, and it is in this state that we are most of the time. Plato teaches moreover that there are many species of pleasure, some of the body and some of the soul.[284] Some pleasures are mixed with their opposites; others remain pure and unmixed. Some owe their existence to memory, others to hope. Some pleasures are shameful, for example, those which occur with intemperance and injustice. Others are moderate and participate in some way or other in the Good, such as the joy produced by good people and the pleasures derived from being virtuous. Since many pleasures are by nature disreputable, we need not even ask if pleasure can be counted among those things that are absolutely good. A pleasure seems to be precarious and, in fact, worthless if it is by nature an accidental accompaniment of something else, contributing nothing essential or fundamental itself, and if it co-exists with its opposite. Pleasure and pain are intermingled, and this would not happen if one were absolutely good and the other absolutely evil.

33

That which deserves most especially and properly to be called friendship is nothing else but that which arises from mutual good will. This happens when each person wants his friend and himself to fare equally well. But this equality cannot be maintained unless their characters are similar. "Like is dear to like when it is moderate, whereas immoderate things are dear neither to one another nor to things moderate."[285] There are also some other relationships

282. *Philebus passim*; *Republic* 585a, *Timaeus* 64c, d.
283. *Philebus* 33a.
284. *Philebus* 32a-d.
285. *Laws* IV 716c, Bury (Loeb).

which have the name friendship although they really are not because they have been merely tinged, as it were, by virtue.[286] For instance, there are the natural feelings parents have for their children and those of relatives for one another. There are also social relationships, and there is camaraderie. These do not always have reciprocity of good will. Love is also in some way a species of friendship. Love can be, on the one hand, honorable if it comes from a virtuous soul, but it can also be base if the soul is wicked; there is also an intermediate type when the soul is neither noble nor ignoble. As there are three states of the soul in a rational animal, good, bad and intermediate,[287] so also there would be three types of love differing one from the other in kind. That there are three types is manifested most clearly by their different goals. Base love is love of the body alone; it has been overcome by pleasure and is therefore brutish.[288] Honorable love exists only for the pure soul in which a suitability for virtue is in evidence. The intermediate type of love desires the body on the one hand and the beauty of the soul on the other. The person who is worthy of love is himself an intermediate sort, neither ignoble nor noble. Hence one must assert that Love personified (Eros) is some sort of divine being rather than a god[289] for gods never assume earthly bodies. Eros transmits to humans gifts from the gods and vice versa. Since love is commonly divided into the three types mentioned above, love that belongs to a good man is free of passion and is a kind of art. It therefore resides in the rational part of the soul. Its goal is to discern who is worthy of love, to take possession of him and embrace him. He judges his beloved by his aims and impulses to see whether they are noble and directed toward the beautiful and whether they are strong and pure. He who strives to possess it will possess it not by corrupting and flattering

286. Letter VII 340d.
287. *Phaedrus* 237d-238c.
288. *Phaedrus* 250e.
289. *Symposium* 202d, e.

the object of his love but rather by exercising restraint and by showing that life is not worth living for a person in the state he is in. And when he wins his beloved, he will pass on to him those things which will make him perfect if he practices them. The end for them will be to become friends instead of lover and beloved.

34

Concerning constitutions Plato says that some cannot be assumed to exist in fact.[290] These he described in the *Republic*. There he first outlined the development of the peaceful city, then that of the city that is feverish and warlike,[291] asking which of these would be better and how it could come to be. The state is divided into three orders very similar to the divisions of the soul;[292] there would be guardians, auxiliaries and craftsmen.[293] To the first of these he grants the power to make decisions and to rule. The second group is to wage war if the need arises. This class is to be compared to the spirited part of the soul and is, as it were, the ally of reason. To the third group he assigns the crafts and the rest of the trades. Plato thinks it necessary that rulers be philosophers and contemplate the highest Good[294] for this is the only way that they will learn to rule the state properly. Human affairs will never be free from evil unless philosophers become kings or those who are called kings by some divine favor become true philosophers.[295] States will not flourish and will not be just until each part abides by its own law[296] so that rulers make decisions for the sake of the people, the auxiliaries serve

---

290. ἀνυποθέτους, "cannot be assumed to exist in fact" Witt; "existent dans l'absolu" Louis.

291. *Republic* 371b-372c, 373a and ff.

292. *Republic* 436a and ff.

293. *Republic* II, III, VI, VII.

294. *Republic* 518b, 533b.

295. Louis comments, "contamination de deux passages: *Republic* 473c, d et Lettre VII 326a, b."

296. αὐτονομῇ, "abides by its own law" Witt.

the rulers and fight on their behalf, and the rest of the people follow obediently. Plato says that there are five types of constitutions;[297] aristocracy exists when the best rule. Secondly there is timocracy in which those who are dominated by motives of ambition[298] rule. In the third place there is oligarchy and after that democracy. Finally there is tyranny, which is the worst of all. Plato also outlines other hypothetical[299] constitutions such as the one in the *Laws* and the one he reviews and corrects in the Letters.[300] He makes use of these constitutions in the *Laws* for cities that are diseased.[301] These have a territory that is well defined and an elite group of men of all ages. It may be fitting for these men to have special upbringing or education or military equipment in accordance with their different natures and locations. Those who dwell by the sea, for instance, would go into navigation and naval combat. Those who live inland would be suitable for the infantry and for weapons that are lighter if they live in the mountains or heavier if they come from rolling plains. Some of the latter could also be in the cavalry. In this type of city he does not decree that women be held in common. Political science is both theoretical and practical, and it seeks above all to make a city good, prosperous, concordant and harmonious. It is an authoritative science[302] and has subject to it the art of war, strategy and the administration of justice. Political science considers a myriad of matters but especially matters of war and peace.

35

I have already said what kind of person the philosopher is. The sophist differs from the philosopher in the first place in his way of

297. *Republic* 543a and ff.
298. "dominated...ambition" Cornford.
299. "which are assumed to be possible" Witt.
300. Letters VII and VIII.
301. *Laws* 628c, d; 636a, 918c, 919b, c.
302. ἐπιτακτική, "authoritative science" Witt.

life in that the sophist earns his living off the young[303] and is willing to be thought honorable rather than to be so. The sophist also differs from the philosopher with reference to subject matter. The philosopher is concerned with things that are always the same and in the same state; the sophist busies himself with non-being, retreating into a domain where it is difficult to see because of the darkness.[304] For non-being is not the opposite of being[305] since non-being does not exist, cannot be conceived and has no real nature, and if a person were obliged to speak of it or think about it, he would refute himself, involving himself in a contradiction.[306] The term non-being, to the extent that it is intelligible, is not a simple negation of being;[307] it has a secondary relationship with something else which is related to being in some way. Thus, unless things participated in non-being, they could not be distinguished from one another. But now, howsoever many beings there are, in that many ways there is also non-being.[308] For that which is not something is not a being.

36

This suffices for an introduction to the teachings of Plato. Some things have perhaps been stated in an orderly way while others have been put forth in a random and illogical manner. In any case, from what has been said it should be possible for anyone to become a student of Plato and consequently be capable of discovering the meaning of the rest of his teachings.

303. *Sophist* 231d.
304. *ibid.* 254a.
305. *ibid.* 257b.
306. *ibid.* 238b.
307. *ibid.* 256d, 259b.
308. *ibid.* 257a.

BIBLIOGRAPHY

Bluck, R. S. *Plato's Phaedo*. London: Routledge & Kegan Paul, 1911.

Burges, G., trans. *The Works of Plato*. 6 vols. London: Henry G. Bohn, 1854.

Bury, R. G. *Timaeus*. Cambridge: Harvard.University Press, 1975.

Cornford, F. M. *The Republic of Plato*. New York: Oxford University Press, 1957.

Dillon, J. *The Middle Platonists: 80 B.C. to A.D. 220*. Ithaca: Cornell University Press, 1977.

Dörrie, H. "Albinos, platonischer Philosoph des 2. Jhdts." *Real-Encyclopädie*, Suppl.-Bd. 12 (1970), 14–22.

Fowler, H. N. *Theaetetus*. Cambridge: Harvard University Press, 1961.

Grube, G. M. A. *Plato's Republic*. Indianapolis: Hackett, 1979.

Hackforth, Reginald. *Plato's Phaedrus*. Indianapolis: Bobbs-Merril, 1952.

Hermann, C. F. *Platonis Dialogi*. 6 vols. Leipzig: Teubner, 1858.

Invernizzi, G. *Il Didaskalikos di Albinos e il medioplatonismo*. 2 vols. Rome: Abete, 1976.

Loenen, J. H. "Albinus' Metaphysics: An Attempt at Reconstruction." *Mnemosyne*, ser. 4, 9 (1956), 296–319 and 10 (1957), 35–56.

Louis, P., ed. *Épitomé*. Paris: Bude, 1945.

Merlan, P. *From Platonism to Neoplatonism*. 3rd. ed., rev. The Hague: Martinus Nijhoff, 1975.

Saunders, Trevor. *Plato, The Laws*. New York: Penguin, 1982.

Witt, R. E. *Albinus and the History of Middle Platonism*. Cambridge: Cambridge University Press, 1937; rpt. Amsterdam: Hakkert, 1971.

PHANES PRESS both publishes and distributes many fine books which relate to the philosophical, religious and spiritual traditions of the Western world. To obtain a copy of our current catalogue, please write:

PHANES PRESS
PO BOX 6114
GRAND RAPIDS, MI 49516
USA